START
WITH
THE END

Living with clarity and purpose

Miriam Indries

Copyright © 2018

All rights reserved. This book or any portion thereof may not be reproduced or used in any manner whatsoever without the express written permission of the author except for the use of brief quotations in a book review.

Printed in Australia
First Printing, 2018
ISBN: 978-0-6483447-6-6

White Light Publishing House
Melton, VIC, Australia 3337
whitelightpublishing.com.au

"This book is dedicated to all the curious souls who are brave enough to leave their comfort zone and explore life as their most authentic self."

PREFACE	7
CHAPTER 1: CIRCUMSTANCES	9
CHAPTER 2: SEE IT	17
CHAPTER 3: FEEL IT	31
CHAPTER 4: BELIEVE IT	41
CHAPTER 5: RESPONSIBILITY	57
CHAPTER 6: COMMITMENT	75
CHAPTER 7: WORK FOR IT	87
CHAPTER 8: THE TOWER MOMENT	99
CHAPTER 9: RELATIONSHIPS AND HEARTBREAK	105
CHAPTER 10: BELONGINGNESS	121
CHAPTER 11: THE WAKE-UP CALL	133
CHAPTER 12: EMOTIONAL BEHAVIOURS	149
CHAPTER 13: THE REBUILDING PHASE	161
CLOSING WORDS	169
LIST OF AFFIRMATIONS	173

PREFACE

In the beginning, we already know the end. From the moment we are born our life purpose reveals itself to us. As the physical body of a baby is introduced to the world for its very first time, in this moment, we know it all: who we are, what the essence of our soul is and most importantly why we are here. So why do we forget as we go through life?

We need to start with the end, to go back within, find the authenticity of our soul and start living with clarity and purpose. No matter what you aspire to be in your life and how much you grow in your social status by chasing professional or personal accomplishments, at some point, you will be reminded of what you were brought here to do and separate from what your ego is asking you to desire. For some this realization will come earlier, and for others, at the end of their physical life when they face the person they were to become. START WITH THE END is a tool and a reminder for you to believe in yourself enough to realise your ability to create and achieve greatness, but to open your heart and connect with your true self because if you are willing to take this journey, it will be an adventure worth exploring.

ONE

CIRCUMSTANCES

My beginning comes from a very humble place. Growing up with very little pushed me towards having bigger dreams. As a child, I wished for many things only to fit in and be like the other kids. I wanted to have the latest Barbie Doll and the best clothes for it, instead of the plastic, fake kind I owned. I remember whenever I used to go and play with the other kids and our Barbies, I always felt so embarrassed yet in a way grateful that I still had a doll. I wanted to have nice clothes like my friends were wearing and bragging about, not to show off, but to be part of the "crew". New clothes for me meant a trip with my mum to the local second-hand shop where I could choose the cheapest of the bunch and go for practicality instead of look.

Don't get me wrong, I was grateful for these, but I must admit they were not always the nicest or the best fit for me. I wanted to go away on exciting family trips during my school holidays and I often dreaded these moments because I knew my time was to be spent at home as we couldn't afford to go anywhere. The last day of school term was always bitter sweet because although I was looking forward to putting away that ugly school uniform, at the same time

I knew that nothing exciting would happen.

My time was to be spent at home and that was the story every time. My colleagues would talk about the exciting plans they had with their families and when my turn came up, I would always make up some sort of story about a wonderful vacation my family and I would go on. I must admit at times I felt odd pretending and making up tales, but I guess that's when I discovered my passion for storytelling. My imagination would lead me to the dreamy experiences I so deeply desired to be part of and although I knew that they would not physically manifest at that moment, I always had a sense of hope and possibility.

I very quickly realised that my desires and my current situation were simply not congruent and so I decided this was not meant to be my life path; that being different was what my life would be about, and I had to learn to get used to it. We had very little money, but the importance of knowledge was always at the forefront of all my life lessons given by my parents. My mother made sure my brother and I got the best bedtime stories and she would often read to us the works of Plato and Aristotle, amongst other brilliant philosophers. I'm pretty sure my curiosity streak developed from here. Perhaps hearing the masterpieces written by these amazing philosophical geniuses inspired me to question everything, but in a good way. I was a dreamer and still am in many ways. Although I didn't have the things others had, what I did possess was something of greater value, which I later on learned about in more depth. I had tons of imagination and the freedom to use it whenever I wanted. My circumstances led to me realise that anything I desired was actually within me and even if at that age, I was unable to comprehend its power, I sure did later on in my life. I remember being eight years old and living in a tiny apartment with my parents and older brother, in an average neighbourhood in Cluj-Napoca, Romania. For those of you who don't know, back then Romania was many great things, but full of opportunities was not one of them. My brother and I were taught to always appreciate everything we had, even though it didn't seem like much. I admit that at times, I could not understand the value of the things we did have, but I still felt a sense of gratitude.

This helped me to clearly identify the true meaning of value, that external and material possessions are nothing but an illusion, and that the true treasures are stored inside us. I decided very early on that I was going to do great things with my life. Perhaps I was motivated by fitting in, or simply wanting to have it all, but I made a pact with myself that I would never have to struggle financially when I grew up and that I would always stand firm on my own two feet, no matter what. I had no idea how I would make this happen because as a child, I didn't yet possess the knowledge I needed to figure it out. And so, I started to mentally create my future experiences because at that age, nothing seemed impossible. I used my current situation as my motivation to wish for better days; the ones I wanted to create for myself. I let my mind and my imagination guide me towards the life I would like to be living. I dreamed that one day I would live in a country with sunny weather, palm trees and a house near the beach. I loved the sound of the waves splashing against the rocks on the shore and even though I had only seen the sea once back then, when I did, something felt like home. I would dream of a having a big wardrobe full of beautiful clothes to call my own. I loved fashion and even though my clothes were not very trendy, I always found a way to make them suit my authentic style. I also dreamt about seeing my parents smile, and to not feel so stressed about their financial problems. Every time I'd see my mother cry, wondering whether we would have enough money to pay the rent that month, I'd force myself to hold back my own tears and instead, picture a moment when money would not be an issue for us, mentally solving the problem in my head.

I began creating my own reality and started to develop a problem-solving mindset, which to me, seemed exciting, even at that young age. My parents fought a lot due to lack of money and although it was painful at the time to see and hear, I decided this was going to be my first great life lesson; it gave me the determination to never let money control my life and to be wiser about picking my future partner when the time came for this. I loved writing and I fantasized that one-day, the world would read my poetry. I began writing poetry from the moment I learnt how to write. It was a way for me to express myself and it was something that came almost naturally to me. Although I wasn't a keen reader, writing was a big part of me.

I often wonder how I came up with all the words to create such deep, poetic works at such a young age, but the only way I could explain it at the time was that it was something inside of me that needed to be heard and putting it on a piece of paper felt like the right thing to do for me. I loved sports and so I often dreamt that I would become a great volleyball player at an international level, amongst the world's greatest (I started the sport at eight years old). My coach was a tough woman who would not stand for any excuses and although our practices were demanding, I loved exploring my competitive side and pushing through the physical pain to become better at the sport. Amongst many other dreams I had, the most prominent one was that one day, I would fly to many beautiful places around the world because to me, this felt like the ultimate freedom. I was a curious kid and I used my mind to transport myself in time to all these amazing experiences I so deeply desired.

I started using my imagination without being aware of its benefits. It brought me so much happiness and it was my exciting escape from the everyday monotonous life I was living. About five years later around the age of thirteen, my parents sat my brother and I down and told us that we would be moving to another country, a place called New Zealand. Whilst high school in Romania was very strict and I knew my geography well, New Zealand was not a place I had ever heard of before. My parents were determined to provide us with a brighter future and that meant living in a different country.

Whilst most kids would miss their friends and the environment they grew up in, for some reason this did not bother me at all. I loved the few friends I had, but change seemed far more exciting to me at that time. I placed so much importance on my dreams and the reality I was constructing for myself, that I had learnt not to get attached to people or places in a way one usually would. I felt an urge to focus so strongly on these and I didn't want anything or anybody to ever get in the way of my dreams.

It is only when I arrived in New Zealand that I realised the power of my thoughts and how my imagination led to reality. I was now living in a hot, sunny place with palm trees nearby a beach. During my high school years, I was awarded the most valuable player in the volleyball team and moved onto playing for regionals. My parents were now in a much better financial situation and were happy, or so it seemed. At the age seventeen, I attended AUT University where I had my first encounter with the fashion industry. One year later, I was working for a top New Zealand fashion designer whilst creating my own brand on the side and selling my clothes in small boutiques. I didn't have a big wardrobe; instead I had my own atelier, full of beautiful fabrics and clothes I designed and made. This was my oasis and I would spend most of my time in it.

At twenty years old, keen to explore more of what life had to offer, I became a flight attendant with one of the best airlines in the world, which was the beginning of a year spent mostly on planes, flying to beautiful places. All the things that I dreamed of as a child were now happening for me. In my mid-twenties, I decided that it was time to do something even more spontaneous, so I bought a plane ticket to the UK, and without knowing what I'd do there, I found myself on March 28 2014, flying 17,000 miles away from home, alone with a suitcase full of clothes and a handbag containing small gifts my friends and family had given me prior to my departure. I spent a few years there, focusing on my career and travelling to many incredible places around Europe.

Whilst I stopped writing poetry once I hit my early teens, I began a blog in my late teenage years that brought me many freelance writing opportunities and a great start to a career in the public relations field. My mother was a well-known journalist in my birth-city and seeing her write stories inspired me to explore the field myself. I was now working with some top journalists in London and for the first time in my life, I felt I was doing something I genuinely loved, and I knew I was exactly where I should be at that time. There is no greater power than the one we can imagine from within. I was only a kid when I began visualizing my desires, which was used as an escape mechanism. I wasn't consciously aware that those things would one day manifest. Little did I know that I had constructed them to be part of my reality because they were already part of me. I had no idea that what I was doing was planting seeds within my universal energetic field and attracting all the experiences I wanted so badly for myself. Or maybe, this was part of my soul's journey, and somehow as a young kid I was able to tap into this incredible knowledge and guidance from within. Regardless of the force that brought me all these amazing experiences, I learnt that even when you are not aware of the power that comes from desiring something, if you imagine it and believe it, and if it's part of your authentic self, then it's possible for you to have it, because within you, you already possess it.

We tend to underestimate our internal power to make things happen and at times, we can forget that we are creators and everything we want, we can actually have. These experiences are already part of us because we see them in our mind. Whether they have happened to us before in a different life our soul ventured on, or represent glimpses of hope of things we wish to move towards, they are still there, in our mind waiting to release themselves. Knowing this now, as an adult, I began wondering… How did I know what I wanted from such a young age? How could I have dreamed of all these beautiful places and experiences without even knowing of their existence? Were they already a part of me?

TWO

SEE IT

Whatever you want for yourself in your life, you must start with the end and that means seeing what the outcome looks like to you. You must first see the bigger picture and explore it from all angles! The human mind has the magical ability to see things that can happen before they actually happen. It's a gift that I believe we all possess; it's the power of our imagination that leads to creation. Consciously creating a clear picture of what your outcome looks like, will give your unconscious mind the direction it needs to follow in order to know where it's going.

To understand this concept, it's important to first comprehend the structure of your mind. There are many different ways of looking at this, but the one I have always used is looking at the mind and its two parts: the conscious and the unconscious. Very self-explanatory, the conscious part of the mind includes every thought, action or feeling that we are consciously aware of. This part is the one we use voluntarily to keep us aware of everything we think, feel and do.

The more complex part is the unconscious, and this is the area of the mind we use involuntarily. Think of it as an autopilot system that controls all processes in order for functioning to be consistent. This part leads our body's functions and it keeps us alive by constantly regulating the bodily systems such as our breathing and heart rate. It is also here that all of our memories are stored. Everything you have done, felt and acquired throughout your life this far had some sort of reaction that created an experience for you and these are all stored within the unconscious part of the mind. You can access your memories at any time but there is something to be mindful of.

The unconscious will sometimes take you by surprise and bring back memories if and when it believes you need to be reminded of these again, and it will also bring unresolved situations when it decides you are ready to face them once again. Have you ever found yourself in the position of remembering a past experience completely at random and then asking yourself why this came to your awareness? Why now? That is how the unconscious mind works, subtly but with certainty, bringing to our present moment something that we thought had long been left in the past. Whilst the mind is a complex yet fascinating system, for this reason it is important to not take it for granted and to work with it constantly so that it can be developed to its full potential.

VISUALIZATION- THE MIND

One of the greatest assets the mind has stems from imagination and it's called visualization. This occurs when you allow your mind to tap into its full potential and use your imagination and cognitive creativity. The great aspect about visualization is that you can do it anytime and it's completely up to you how you use it. All that's required of you is to figure out what you want and start seeing it as if it's already happening for you. There are no limitations when it comes to this, as our imagination is limitless so let it guide you to create the picture you'd like to see. I am sure that most of us would have used visualization many times in our life, perhaps not even being aware that we are doing so.

But for achieving goals, visualization is one of the key factors that should be mastered in order to gain a clear perspective of what it is you are trying to achieve and how this achievement actually looks like in its completed, full state. Just as we use programs like Photoshop to construct and edit images, visualization is like software of the brain used to mentally create images that you decide based on your aspirations, your goals and your soul's true essence. It's like a Polaroid picture created in your mind and available to you whenever you want to use it. You can create images and also edit and change them based on what you actually want them to look like.

You could even look at it as a super power you possess, one that if you devote your time to elevate, it will guide you towards what you are really seeking. The more you practice, the better you get at it so discipline and commitment are vital in order to develop it. And once you get better at it, it will come naturally to you. Have you ever wondered why some people can see things so clearly, and when they are faced with a dilemma they simply just see the solution instead of all the conundrums? What are they doing differently? How can they have the ability to surpass those roadblocks and just see freely the highway ahead? The answer is simple; they figured out the best way to use their mind and that is by simply allowing it to be whilst staying in control of it guided from within.

However, some people don't necessarily feel they are in control of their own mind and cannot manage to access their internal cues. In this instance, their mind is in a constant dilemma of associating past experiences with present reactions or looking into the future instead of focusing in the now and what is actually real in the present time. All these different situations confuse them greatly to the point they lose the ability to focus and sooner or later fall in the trap of saying "That's life, it is how it is". This happens when fear comes into play.

The unconscious part of the mind will always look for ways to keep you safe and comfortable, and it does this very cleverly by bringing back past experiences that have a relevant point to your present moment. By doing so, you will instantly associate your current situation with what once was and find yourself confused about what is in the now. It can also do so with future references, such as tricking you into postponing something until a later date, which is otherwise known as procrastination, one of the many consequences stemming from fear. It does so to keep you comfortable by not allowing you to get outside of your comfort zone because the unknown frightens your ego.

However, if we look at time as an illusion, the past and future are simply non-existent. You might have heard successful entrepreneurs and motivational speakers talk about how everything began happening for them as soon as they started taking action and together with their biggest fears, they moved towards what they believed in.

The great Les Brown once said that "You don't have to be great to get started but you do have to get started to be great". The greatness we all possess can only come alive when we create a shift in the mind to believe and work towards it. Fear as we will learn in later chapters is and will always be part of us, and we can actually use it to our advantage instead of seeing it as the great big enemy.

AWARENESS - THE SOUL

Whilst the brain is the physical element of our existence that guides our thoughts and behaviours, there is also a non-physical aspect, and that is the soul. Beyond our physical existence, we are energetic beings brought together in a bigger energetic field we call the universe. Like the mind, the soul has its own intelligence by how it functions, and it often communicates with us through our intuition. The soul is limitless and has endless potential.

It can travel in time over and over again and its flexibility allows it to become part of new physical bodies as it is chosen to do so. The soul is the part of ourselves that holds the key to our purpose, the infinite possibilities, the "why" we are here. When we are in tune with our energetic internal field, we connect with our purest essence, with the most authentic part of ourselves. The closer you get to the soul and align your mind, physical body and actions with its intention, the more in tune you become with who you really are and what you are here for.

Remember, we all once knew this, but along the way we forgot because as we grow in age and experiences, the more distractions we become aware of. We all have a purpose to fill and this is the greatest treasure every person on this planet holds. Our unique ability to provide and bring value to the world in our own way is greatly influenced by the soul and its mission. Sometimes we may find ourselves in situations that simply do not feel right. On paper they add up, but somewhere deep down within us, there is a small twinge of doubt or confusion that makes us question it. This is the voice of the soul, its way of communicating with us to advise us if we are on the right path or if we need to slightly change its course to get back on it. Life is as much about the side streets as it is about your "final" destination. The problem many of us face though is that the moment we get lost, we start turning on the wrong side streets instead of taking a moment to listen to our inner guidance and assess the path ahead. We rush into things out of desperation, maybe because of the feeling of adventure we get, or perhaps fear gets in the way, so we try to escape and run away.

What we often don't see is that there is no escape in this is life and its beauty lies within these parameters of back and forwards movement. It is these conundrums that will help us grow and expand our vision to seeing new ways to get to where we are meant to be. Feeling doubtful can actually be a blessing, because when you start to question why you are doing what you are doing, you begin to realize this is your way of connecting with your true source, the soul and so you are ready to receive its messages.

These are important messages that we should always pay attention to. Our intentions are the guidance we need in order to move forward and travel on the path we are meant to be on. Most of us know or remember that path, but we choose to ignore it or have done so for so long that we no longer have the clarity to see it as it is.

When you feel stuck, just think about your motives and if they are aligned with your instinctual existence, you will continue the journey on your right path no doubt.

MEDITATION

If you have practiced mediation before, you will have a better understanding of what it is. I actually believe everybody has practiced meditation at some point in their life. Whether you were aware of it or not, the practice itself happened.

Meditation is the practice of being present in the moment and being aware of all that's around you, without actually reacting to any of it. Our minds are constantly switched on, throwing thoughts at us every moment of every day. Most of the time, without us being aware of this, we react almost instantly to anything that challenges our thoughts and feelings, whether it comes from external or internal sources. Through meditation, we are aware of everything; we can clearly focus on our breathing patterns, feel our heartbeat, smell all scents around, and feel all physical sensations and yet we can just accept these as they are without needing to react or change anything. Meditation teaches us to be still and stay present in the moment, with no need to be in control, but instead to just let ourselves immersed in the now.

Remember that our unconscious mind is the part that controls all of the body's functions, and because these are involuntary automatic actions, we rarely pay attention to them. Consciously, in everyday life, we devote our attention solely to one sense at a time, sometimes a couple. But when you are in a deep, meditative state you become aware of all senses working in flow together and if you sit still for long enough, you can really experience and appreciate these magical states we often take for granted. When this happens, your physical self will connect deeper with your energetic self and this brings your awareness to your authenticity and personal power. When you can sit still for a moment, feel your energy and remain fully conscious of this whilst in a peaceful state, you are experiencing a meditative state. In this moment, you feel truly alive because all you know is the present and nothing else; you are simply living in the now, the only tense that truly matters! Although this may seem easy to achieve, meditation requires regular practice. It's easy to externalize everything, but when you have to go inwards and really look at what lies deep within you or outside of you without reacting but simply becoming aware of it, this takes courage, patience and a lot of hard work. I was never able to fully understand this concept until I began meditating.

I had always been intrigued by the mind and our sense of identity and have always been open to holistic practices to understand these even further. When I finished my psychology studies I was fascinated with science, but I was even more curious to find the truth from a holistic side also. This led me to my Ayurveda studies and Chinese medicine, the two oldest medical systems in the world, in the hopes of understanding how these practices explained the mind and body. During my Ayurveda studies, I was introduced to the meaning of consciousness and different ways of tapping into it such as yoga and meditation. I began with guided mediation and slowly shifted to self-meditation. Guided meditation can actually help you learn to become still and focus on what you are hearing, whilst going in a deeper relaxed state to the point that your attention is switched solely to the person's voice that's guiding you. In such state, you become fully present. Guided meditation can be your initial step into the practice itself. Whilst this is great to start with and certainly very helpful, the true beauty and purity of meditation begins during the time you are able to use your own guidance and connect inwards without needing to be externally guided.

I still remember my first self-meditation so well. I was living in Brighton, UK at the time and I had just broken up with my boyfriend. I thought I was at peace with my decision about letting go of that relationship, but something inside of me felt turbulent and confusing. I wasn't sure if this was due to the aftermath of the break up or something much deeper. I make most decisions based on my gut feel, and whilst my instinct agreed with it, something else was resisting this break-up. Being the curious person I am, I decided to seek the answers from within. I knew that I needed to stop analyzing all that was going on and tap into my purest essence, which meant disconnect from all cognitive and emotional distractions and connect solely with my soul.

I lay myself down on the floor; I still remember it being a very cold winter's day, with heavy rain outside. The heater's warm air was venting on my resting body and after a moment of settling down on the soft carpet, I closed my eyes. I lay there for about 10 minutes with nothing actually happening. I wasn't sure of what I was expecting to happen, but my mind was clearly still very much guiding me to think and create expectations. I was frustrated and felt a little bit silly to be honest; I could hear my house mates downstairs talking and laughing, and thought to myself "What am I doing laying on the floor on my own?" I was just about to give up when something finally completely switched off for me. In this moment, everything else went completely blank and I began seeing a vision of myself climbing some very steep stairs. It almost felt like lucid dreaming because I was aware of it, but I just couldn't stop this process. I wanted to see where those stairs were taking me and all of a sudden, I began seeing different pictures and snippets of experiences, some making sense, some completely disjointed from what I knew so far of my life.

I felt completely immersed in this experience; it's as if I was watching a film without knowing what was to come next. I saw myself working in an office with an orange wall; I saw myself walking on a beach in a place I had never seen before although the vision of it was very clear; and then I was on a plane travelling somewhere arriving at an airport with a very distinct look; I saw all these happenings and although I couldn't relate to them nor had I seen these places, I felt a slight familiarity with them. It's as if I had been there before but I didn't, not in this lifetime at least.

I lay there for about 30 minutes but to me it felt like time stood still. A few moments after, I became aware of all that was happening around me and I instantly opened my eyes. In that moment, something changed for me. Although I felt exhausted, my decision was confirmed and I felt completely at peace. It was clear to me that the break-up was lead from within, but my confusion was due to my ego's fear of being single and alone. I wish I could describe the feeling of it all, but it was something that perhaps makes no sense to put into words because it simply does not fit within the dimension our physical conscious states recognize.

It was to this day, the most powerful meditative state I had ever reached and an experience I will never forget. Two years later, I started working in a company that had the exact same orange wall as the one introduced to me in my mediation. You make the call…

Meditation manifests itself in different ways, but at its core as I had learned, that connection you will gain with your source, your true soul and spirit, will provide you with signs and insight into where you are at in your life, where you have been or where you are headed.

It's important to allow your mind to tap into its full power and connect with your soul. It is then that clarity will come naturally. You might not get a visual result from your meditation practice, but you will no doubt feel the guidance. If you open your soul, it will show you what you are meant to see. The soul is ethereal, we can't see it, we can't touch or point at it, but we can feel it and that's more powerful than anything else we experience. The soul is honest and pure, and it knows you better than you consciously know yourself.

Having a clear mind will allow your aspirations to come to life and your imagination to flourish. When you are setting yourself up for any goal, using your imagination is the most powerful way to explore that sight and discover its true meaning to you, before it happens.

The beautiful thing about doing so during a meditation session is simply because even though you are aware of it, you are not actively guiding everything with your mind, but instead your energy becomes activated and the guidance now comes from a much deeper place.

THREE

FEEL IT

The universe is a magical place. I say magical because we are magicians, the creators of our own lives. We can use our imagination to transport us in time, to any given moment or place. We can use our emotions to feel whatever we want to feel. Life itself may be limited in time for our physical self, but our souls will forever embrace the nature of being alive, of being creative and full of hope and divine guidance. Through our physical self, we can make anything happen but only when we align ourselves with the spiritual, energetic self. Our souls will forever shine their brightness and it is our ultimate purpose to manifest this brightness into the physical dimension we have come to experience.

The universe is a magical place because we can ask and we will receive. We don't always get it when we want it or even how we imagined it exactly, but the feeling it will bring from whatever manifests itself will always be congruent with the one of our initial desire. With every breath we take, we activate the vibrational frequency between our energetic self and the one of the universe. We are one with the universe, we are the magicians, and we are the souls that long to create, communicate and fulfil a purpose that was once given and will forever live on and shine its brightness. Matters of the heart are amongst some of the most powerful sensations the human body can experience. When you feel something, in that moment you simply become one with it. Feelings are so powerful that they can create major shifts in our life.

Many of the situations we react to are unconsciously driven by our emotional states, which in turn are manifested by the events that occur externally and internally. Just like the calm before the storm ideology, we can feel relaxed one moment but when something comes and interferes with this, our emotions change which causes a reaction. Therefore, we could say that the emotional self and the cognitive self are a team and when they work together, everything runs smoothly, but when one goes against the other, a state of imbalance occurs between the two and tension is created which leads us to release it, often done so in a reactive state.

For this to happen there has to be something that triggers it. This could be anything from an event, to a feeling you once felt, to a particular type of person you are interacting with. Everything you have gone through in your life so far has been recorded in your brain's memory box compartment. The unconscious part of your mind is like a hard drive that has unlimited storage, so it all gets safely stored in there.

If for example at one point in your life, you reacted emotionally in a strong way to a particular situation, this could also be stored within your unconscious. And every time you encounter a similar situation, your brain will almost instantly remember that past experience and start to react similarly. This is not always the case and sometimes your reaction will need to have had some sort of impact on your behavior, but it can happen. For example, every Sunday morning, I love going to my local café and get a cup of coffee whilst reading the newspaper. Every time I go there, the customer service is amazing and I feel very relaxed.

So, my experience has been recorded as pleasant. Regardless how my day is going, whenever I go to that particular café I feel relaxed instantly. My brain has created a learned response, and this is that the café is associated with a feeling of being relaxed. The same could go for a negative situation. One of my dearest friends has a big phobia of airports. Phobias are in many cases a learned response that occurs in a particular situation and environment in which one negative situation triggered a strong reaction and so the negative experience has been recorded in the mind. My friend's fear of airports developed in her late teens when she went on a holiday with her family. It was a very hot day and the queue was long. She didn't have any water with her and was feeling quite dehydrated. Not thinking much of it, she continued to wait in the queue and twenty minutes later she fainted.

From then onwards, she was afraid that every time she will step in an airport she will faint. Whilst chances of this happening are very slim, her previous experience however made such a big impact for her that she began associating airports with feeling ill and fainting. And so whenever she entered an airport, her mind would remind her of that particular incident and fear would start kicking in.

According to the *NLP (neuro linguistic programming) model developed by Dr Richard Bandler, the human brain has three ways in which it processes information. It either deletes it, distorts it or generalizes it. This is a way for us to filter through the information, which suits our own model of the world or one that helps us create our perception of our own reality. In the examples above, we can say that the situations are generalized perhaps in a way that I associate that specific café with tranquillity, or that my friend has a generalized internal model about airports and fainting. Whilst I could continue writing from referencing the great geniuses of the psychology field or other models such as the NLP one, let's just keep things simple.

If we believe something will happen again and we associate a feeling to it, whether it's fear, love, happiness, joy, disgust and so on, we will always expect our behaviour to follow from this. It makes sense then to start associating a feeling to a particular goal you have so that its impact will be more powerful, and you will manifest this in your life.

Have you ever found yourself reacting to something in a negative way, maybe you got snappy with your colleague for something they said or did, even though it had no reference to you? Then shortly after, you felt slightly confused and asked yourself why you reacted so strongly about this as it wasn't even related to the reason why you reacted. In that moment, your emotional state could have been calm but your ego may have taken personally what they said so you instantly went into a defensive state and quickly reacted. The ego will always aim to keep us safe and because it takes everything personally, if you lead with your ego, very rarely you can make sound decisions that align with your core authentic self.

I, like many other people, have quite a sensitive nature and am a passionate soul. A born LEO star sign, naturally I lead with my heart. For me it's very easy to get worked up over something I feel strongly or passionate about. Although sometimes this can be a good thing, certain situations require patience and processing of information. I have lived most of my life in an inpatient state. Because of my fiery nature, when I wanted something I wanted it then and if it didn't happen as I wanted it, I would get stressed out, restless and in a state of panic. Because of this, I have learnt and continue to adapt so that I can balance my emotions out because I realized that too much of something can be detrimental to my overall well-being. I especially noticed this when I was working as an Ayurveda practitioner and had clients who were experiencing various health problems.

Some came to see me in regard to their digestion problems, whilst others were experiencing anxiety, stress and depression. Through the consultation process, I realized that sometimes these were to do with the person's emotional state and that meant their vibrational field would meet with mine. Regardless of the circumstances, when two people meet and are in close proximity of one another, the souls connect on an energetic level. This causes the energies to vibrate towards one another and often when one is stronger than the other, energy can be transferred from between the two people.

I had to find a way in which they would be able to release their emotional difficulties without directly interfering with my energy, but simply externally. Most healers who work with energy will have a way of protecting their own energy, and this was something I had to learn to do also. We must always protect our own energy first before we invite others to share theirs with us. I discovered in doing so that we can be selective over what actually affects us emotionally and to the degree it does so. During my first year of studying psychology, my mind was in complete overload. I was striving to be the best student and get straight A's not only because that is in my nature but also because I loved the subject.

My introduction to the studies of the human mind and how it affects behaviour was highly pleasant. I loved psychology and was absolutely fascinated with the amount of discoveries made over the years and how these came to be. I was intrigued about the psyche and how it affects our overall functioning, and I found myself in complete awe with every single lesson learnt. At one point, I decided I was going to become a clinical psychologist, but this was very quickly turned down during my third year of studying when I realized the entry criteria was simply not congruent with the subjects nor the grades I was getting. I felt defeated and like a complete loser. How could I not make it I said to myself? Shame on me for all the time wasted studying and here

I was not even able to move forward with my goals I thought I wanted to achieve at the time. I let this feeling of unworthiness get to me so much to the point that I lost my passion for what I loved doing. I even thought about quitting my studies because it all felt pointless to me if I was not able to get to my desired destination. But after two and a half years of intense learning I decided I would stick to it and complete my degree. There was no way I was going to let something like this affect my determination. I switched my brain back to the problem-solving mode to find a solution. I began digging in deep to find out all the reasons why I did want to become a clinical psychologist to begin with. This meant I had to take time by myself, to question my reasons and find a solution.

I wrote down on a piece of paper things like "I want to help and empower people, I want to work in a field that requires continuous learning; I enjoy research; I want to work with people from all walks of life".

Clarity quickly came over me and I realized that clinical psychology was not the only path for me to be able to do all those things. All of a sudden, I came up with different areas of study that I could explore further, which all would lead me to a new outcome. And I am certainly thankful I did, because looking back now I can honestly say clinical psychology is not the career I would have enjoyed pursuing in the end. Somewhere deep within me, my soul's energy was vibrating away from what I thought I wanted and the universe picked up this vibration and planted a small roadblock in my way so that I could reassess what was actually the path I should strive towards.

What I have learned over time so far in my life is that regardless how much you want something, you must identify if that something is actually right for you. We can enjoy so many things, but to make it into something sustainable, you also need to be very honest with yourself and see what you are actually good at doing and what will serve you for the best. And if you ignore the feeling, the universe will interfere and create a way in which you get it or not, depending on the situation and its impact on your life. I thought clinical psychology was what I wanted, but I didn't listen to what I was feeling. I just pursued it based on what "was required" for me in order to achieve all the things that I wanted to do. Deep down, I didn't feel happy about it, I just felt like it was the thing I had to do.

But when I discovered a more holistic approach to my goals it felt 100% right to me and as I began studying Ayurveda I felt in that moment completely aligned with my deepest soul's desire. And so, it proved to be the right path to embark on. It can be difficult at times to separate what the heart wants from what your mind wants. Thinking is rational and offers no openness beyond logic, but to feel, that's something completely different, something we cannot control.

I'm not saying you should always let yourself guided by your heart, some situations require more of a rational approach, whilst most situations need to be looked at from all angles, emotional, metal and spiritual. But it's good to be aware of your feelings. As the soul often communicates with our physical state through our intuition, this is a feeling and it should never be ignored. Self-awareness is about being in tune with yourself as a whole.

FOUR

BELIEVE IT

In my mid-twenties, when I took the spontaneous decision to move across to the other side of the globe, to the UK I had absolutely no idea what I was going to be doing or where I was going to stay. Something within pushed me to get outside of the boring, rut I was living back in New Zealand. Don't get me wrong, I had a somewhat beautiful life, but I didn't necessarily feel content. My friends were great; I had my family close and I was working in a job that offered me great financial stability for that stage in my life.

But as you may have already figured out by now, money was never something that brought me true happiness because I had lived a big part of my life without it, so its effects were not that important to me. Although I was aware that money can make everything easier, I also knew it can complicate things. I had already experienced both the positive and negative effects money can have on one's lifestyle, so I learnt to recognize the true value of something not through its financial worth but through the possibilities and sentimental value it would bring.

For most of my time in New Zealand, my love life was almost non-existent because even though a part of me wanted to be in a beautiful romantic relationship, most of me desired much more than that and on a completely different path. I decided love would have to wait because my dreams were much more important to me!

When I needed love, I learnt to give it to myself and quickly discovered that when you love yourself for who you are, love vibrates all around you from many different people and most importantly, from the universe itself. I had come to appreciate that there is no greater love than the one I had with myself and the universe around me. What I wanted was adventure and a glimpse of something that would help me expand myself mentally, emotionally, physically and spiritually. I felt an urge to unleash all this potential I recognized I had, and I knew that New Zealand was not going to offer me the discomfort I required in order to find my inner power.

I had become uncomfortable with the feeling of being comfortable and this brought a great uneasiness to my life. My life seemed out of balance to me. I found myself doing the same things, with the same people, in the same places and this quickly became a cycle I was no longer able to take part in. At the same time, I felt grateful to be living in a country that offers so much freedom and beautiful landscapes. The beach walks with my dog Max, the late night barbeques with my friends, and Sunday brunch on the deck with my family; these were all beautiful experiences that will forever be in my heart, but my soul was ready for an adventure and so was the rest of me. I still remember the moment I arrived at Gatwick airport. It was my first time in the UK and I have never travelled on my own before. Dragging my ridiculous pink suitcase set around the airport, lost without knowing where to go, I had to simply sit still for a moment and appreciate it all. The levels of excitement I was experiencing were balanced out by a fear that came over me.

This was a great moment; because it was then I sat with my fear, acknowledged it and took the conscious decision to face the storm. I knew that I had already taken the hardest step, and that was to actually leave New Zealand and all that has been so dear to me so I was somewhat feeling confident with my ability to deal with what was to come for me on this adventure. Looking around the busy airport, I could see hundreds of people rushing everywhere. You only really notice the chaos inside an airport when you just sit still and absorb it all and I was doing exactly that, one could say I was in the middle of a storm.

Some of these people were running towards their loved ones in the arrivals lounge with tears in their eyes; others were rushing to get outside of the airport and smell the fresh air of their new destination; I saw no familiar faces or places for that matter, and this made me feel scared. I had nobody to run to and hug and in that moment, I began to take responsibility for my life completely.

There I was, alone and so far away from my loved ones, the place I had called home for so many years. In a way, it was all I knew and everything now seemed foreign and unknown. The fear I was feeling was of a unique kind; it felt as though it was a motivation to push me further because I had already come so far; 17,000 miles to be exact. I had no security of where I would be staying, what I was going to do or how I would even get the bus into town. It's as if I had pressed the reset button in my life, but this time I was a 25-year-old newborn. I felt vulnerable but nonetheless courageous. Being away from my comfort zone was proving to be better than I had expected. I loved the feeling of needing to be responsible and the independence my new life provided me with.

I felt excited about my new adventure and what made me so sure about it was the belief I had in myself about this new chapter of my life. The drive and motivation I had since I was a little girl in Romania were burning deeper within me at this point. I had finally taken a big step forward and looking back was no longer an option

I knew if I trusted myself, I would achieve great things here. People often say that moving away on your own is hard because you will never feel at home again, but I discovered that home is actually where you decide it is. And when you trust yourself completely you will find the inner peace you need to call any place you find yourself in, your home.

Because as I was about to learn, home is within yourself and this trip brought me back home, to know, accept and love myself unconditionally. I learnt that my validation was the only one that mattered and so long I believed in myself, all was going to be well. That's the thing about being on your own, you start to notice your greatest strengths and weaknesses and have no choice but to work on them so that you can be a better version of you; because when you're vulnerable and starting brand new, the only person you can trust is yourself. And when you do so, everything will fall into place as it is meant to.

I am a big believer in trusting your intuition and following your heart. The best advice I ever got was from my gut, and when something felt right or wrong it turned out to be true. When you can find inner peace by aligning your emotional self with your spiritual self and your cognitive self, you end up in a state of balance that is more powerful than you would ever think. It is in these moments that you become you, re-discover yourself and when your authenticity comes to light.

I believed that I will find my dream job here and I would excel in everything I wished for. At times, I wondered if I was being slightly delusional, especially when the first job interview I went for was an instant rejection. But I came out of that knowing it was not the right one for me, and contrary to how I would previously react to a similar situation, I felt a sense of empowerment that I deserved more.

When you believe the universe has great plans for you and no matter what goes, you will realize that things happen for you not to you. Two days later, I had a call from a different company, for a job I had applied for before I actually arrived in the UK. I had no reply from them until now and I didn't think too much of it. But here I was, taking a phone call from their HR department who asked if I could go for an interview immediately. Feeling tired and jetlagged, I got in a taxi and went for my first interview with them, and two days later, I was advised I got the job. I'm not sure how I knew this, but I was certain this was something that will completely change my life forever; and later on, I was yet again proven to be right about my intuition.

Once you have visualized where it is you are going, you have broken the seal; that small bump that was stopping you from elevating to a whole new level. We all possess three powerful resources that nobody can take away: the mind, the imagination and the passion. When you start using your mind to its full potential, believe in your imagination and team this up with the passion you have for making it happen, you best believe it's possible. Imagination leads to creation, so you need to believe in your imagination enough to take the action towards its creation. In order to manifest amazing things for yourself, you have to believe in them 100%. Trusting yourself and your abilities is a pivotal feature you must hold onto once you find it. When you start to truly believe in what you are setting yourself up for, you bring emotion into it and with this comes passion.

Emotional states are extremely powerful especially when it comes to desires and goals you'd like to achieve in your life; the stronger your emotional states align themselves with your goals, the higher heights you shall reach. When you believe it, you are directing your unconscious mind to start working towards it; you are making it real and its potency will start reflecting through your actions. Always remember that your unconscious mind has no idea what's true and what's false; it just knows what you tell it. So the more you tell it something you really want, the more it becomes a fact and it goes so deep into its roots that your emotions start to be involved. Once this happens, you will feel its force because it then becomes part of your whole being. Your reality will now include this possibility because you have chosen to believe that you can do it.

SELF-LIMITING BELIEFS

Everything we hold to be true to ourselves, it simply is. Whatever you tell yourself is possible or not possible, it is the truth because it's what you believe in; and this is what creates your reality. Henry Ford said that "If you think you can do a thing or you think you can't do a thing, then you are right." This simple statement is one of the most important quotes I will remind myself of whenever I reach times of doubt. It is a reminder that whatever I think will happen, eventually it will. Beliefs can be of all kinds, some will push us towards better things whilst others will impede us from growing and exploring further. Self-limiting beliefs are just that; thoughts you believe to be true which limit you to take the action required in order to make your desired reality come happen. They can be created based on your previous experiences, what you hear from others, things you have seen, situations you encounter throughout your life. Every day, from the moment we wake up until we go back to sleep, we go through different experiences. Some we choose to acknowledge, whilst others we completely ignore. But they all have an influence on you, on your beliefs and therefore your behaviour. When you believe something is true for you, it will transmit through your behaviour. Bob Proctor said that "if you want to know what your primary thoughts are, simply look at the results you are getting". The unconscious mind plays a leading role in this because it is the part of the mind that controls your emotions. And when your beliefs become attached to emotion, they become stronger and more influential towards your behaviour.

Based on these, you will start taking action according to what you hold to be true for yourself and your reality. When you resist an action towards a desired goal it is most likely because of fear that took part in shaping the self-limiting beliefs you have created. Unfortunately, without you consciously realizing, you are actually stopping yourself from achieving great things and taking on new opportunities. Self-limiting beliefs are simply a way for you to trip yourself up on the road that leads you to your desired destination. You are choosing to fall because you are telling yourself you will do so. In order to believe in yourself, you must absolutely know that you are capable and that what you want is in fact possible. When you are able to do this, you will no longer require validation from anybody else but yourself. You are the one who decides how you live your life and to believe in yourself, you must acknowledge this.

This is the most powerful kind of thinking and indeed it is attainable to those who are brave enough to open their heart to themselves, which then further expands to the universe and those around you.

To explore self-limiting beliefs even further, let's look at the three most commonly known ones that people choose to experience throughout their lifetime. I came across these during my *neuro-linguistic programming studies and they have completely helped me re-evaluate the way I was thinking and realize how I was actually creating limitations for myself.

1. "I CAN'T DO THIS"

Have you ever said to yourself that you can't do something you really wanted to do? I know you have, I have too, and so has everybody else. When you say to yourself you can't do something, what you are really doing is eliminating all possibility. You have created a belief about your situation and you are certain you simply cannot do whatever it is that you'd like to do.

Once you have decided this, you will need to prove to yourself that you are right and so you will begin making up excuses to validate your belief. These could include statements like" I don't have the money to start my own business, I don't have time for a relationship, I can't go to university because I am too old, I can't go travelling because I can't fly on my own, I can't run a marathon because I'm not fit enough, I can't cook, I can't do that presentation, I can't get that job… I could keep going on, but I think the point I am trying to make is clear enough. What you are doing here is limiting your opportunities because you are giving into your fear. It's easy to say you can't do something and then go back to living comfortably, without having to actually find a solution. You are infesting your brain with excuses to support your limiting belief and guess what? You believe it's true! What you need to look at is breaking this pattern and turning the "I can't" into"I am able to".

You can start shifting your thoughts to statements such as "I am able to start my own business and I will use all my resources to gain the financial stability it requires; I am able to run that marathon and I will train consistently in order to bring up my fitness levels; I am able to go back to university and study what I love and all I need to do is fill in that application form and create a plan". If you start telling yourself that you are able to something and you identify the solution for it, you are opening up the possibility that you can make anything you want to happen because you have the ability to do so.

In the moments when you start challenging your mind, that's when your fear will become even stronger. This is when that self-doubt is created and you start questioning yourself. This is completely normal and painful at the same time. But once you break that limitation that's been holding you back, you will have the possibility of elevating to a whole new level and with a little bit of courage, you will never have to return to these limitations again. There have been many times in my life when I let my limitations stop me from reaching the things I wanted. And for years I told myself that it was ok, blaming everybody else, blaming my environment and pretty much everything else but myself. However, when I discovered that I was sabotaging myself, I made the conscious decision to break this. I wanted to live with integrity and feel reliable on myself, and to do this I had to work on myself first and my thinking patterns. It wasn't easy, but once I overtook some of these self-created roadblocks, I saw more clearly and possibilities were now opening themselves to me.

2. "I'M NOT WORTHY OF THIS"

Have you ever wanted something so badly but deep down you always believed you were actually not worthy of it? Let's just say you wanted to get into a relationship with a wonderful person who has achieved great things both personally and professionally, but you told yourself that this kind of person will never look at you that way because you are not good enough, that you don't reach their standards. This is a limiting belief that you created for yourself. You've decided in your mind you are not worthy of being with somebody like that and now you have come to believe it. And then you fall deeper into the cycle of despair. The more you tell yourself you are not worthy, to more you push yourself towards believing it and this creates your reality. Then you will find yourself experiencing situations that are not congruent with your true authentic self, because the intention you put out in the universe was of unworthiness of good things. When you don't believe you are worthy of something, you are de-valuing yourself and with this, failing to recognize all your amazing qualities that actually make you just as worthy as anybody else.

But if you don't trust yourself and believe this is true, then you will end up living a life where you believe are not worthy of doing the things you want to be doing. What you ask for, you will receive. The universe makes no compromise or special detours so you need to be mindful of the things you choose to desire and the self-worth you put out there. You are worth so much; your life is a gift and you were born with a purpose; your existence adds value to the world, but you just need to start believing this. Look at your strengths, focus on all you have done so far that you are proud of and made you happy at some point.

Spend time with yourself and start enjoying your own company to see just how valuable your presence really is. Look within, and not externally, because that is where the most attention needs to be paid. When you start looking internally and bring the light to the storm that's been brewing in there, you will find that your worthiness is there, waiting for you to acknowledge and take it, because once you find it, accept it and embrace it, you find out what really makes you. Your soul is full of kindness and it holds the authentic power and creativity you are meant to bring to this world.

Why waste that for some selfish thoughts of self-doubt and pity? Why create a problem when there is none? Take your mind out of the equation, remove all thinking, just feel and breathe. In a moment like this, you may find yourself seeing the clarity, the one you once held and let go away. Create your thoughts to illuminate your path and not darken it, for it is the light you possess within you that will bring out your worth.

3. "I DON'T DESERVE THIS"

Take a moment and go back as far as you can remember, to a time when you were just a young kid with lots of dreams. Did you feel invincible? Did something stop you from believing you deserve to grow up and be who you want to be? Your answer is probably no because in your younger days, you hardly focused on self-limiting beliefs. The concept was too complex for to understand and that age. Back then, you were probably more aligned with your soul's purpose and this is why when we are young, we believe all is possible. Your imagination is more powerful than you think and at that stage, all you are doing is actually using all your resources instead of crowding your mind with limitations because they simply don't exist. Telling yourself you don't deserve something is like waking up every morning and not getting out of bed for the rest of the day.

You are lying there, awake and are alive but are you really living?

Are you using your resources, your body, your mind, your imagination and your passion? Are you productive to the point that you realize what you are good at and what you deserve because you put the hard work in it? You need to start being kind to yourself and to the life you have been given. Learn to acknowledge your unique self and be just that! You deserve everything you want to create for yourself and more, and all you have to do is make the choice to make it happen. Only when you start understanding what you deserve, then you will get it. Those who seek receive and those who hide will eventually be found.

So regardless what path you choose to take, at one point in your life, you will need to face yourself and realize what you deserve. This is the only way to get closer to the real you. Ask yourself what is stopping you from believing you deserve it? Start now; don't waste any more time and energy into negative beliefs that have trapped you into an empty bubble of misery.

Tell yourself daily affirmations that reflect your desires and worth such as: "I deserve to live an abundant life; I deserve happiness and love; I deserve that pay rise; I deserve to have a family." When you decide this, you will start to feel it and believe it.

But you must value your worth so much so, that you put in the work to confirm it to yourself. Whilst you should never rely on others to heighten your awareness of how amazing you really are, you do need to rely on yourself. With this comes action, and the behaviors you take. Relying on yourself means that you will do what you said you will. When your actions are congruent with your reliability, you will start believing that you deserve it.

You don't need a magic wand for you to know your life can be truly prosperous and abundant. What you do need is to start using your mind, imagination and passion towards the things you know will bring more beauty in your life. Remember your self-limiting beliefs are simply statements you create for yourself; they are only true because you perceive them to be! They are simply just sentences you make up to create excuses for what you are so afraid to reach out to.

FIVE

RESPONSIBILITY

From a young age, I felt a sense of deep responsibility for myself. My parents were kind and loving towards me and I felt accepted by my peers. But I also felt like an outsider as I was an independent kind of a soul. In a way, I would say I was a strange kid because I wasn't necessarily interested in the activities other kids would be excited about. I would get bored easily and routine would soon turn into a monotonous kind of living for me. Writing however was my passion and as a child I would sit for hours in my room writing poetry. In fact, my mother reminded me one day in my twenties that as a kid I would feel more entertained being in my room writing instead of being out with the other kids playing with my dolls even though for short periods of time, that was fun also.

I just remember being so fascinated with the idea of creating something out of nothing, and so the blank paper would soon be filled with poetry my 7-year-old brain could come up with. As the years went by, I developed my creative writing into a more mature kind and I began creating little booklets for my mother on her birthday with inspirational sayings I came up with.

I felt that if I was going to achieve my dreams, I would have to start then. At that age, of course I wasn't aware of motivational speakers, but small sayings of hope would flow out of me and onto the piece of paper, and somehow it would turn into a beautiful small book that put a smile on my mother's face. To this day, writing feels the most natural to me and somehow, I knew then that I had to take responsibility for my own actions and just continue writing.

The first time I was properly introduced to responsibility in regard to elevating to a whole new level in my career was during my stay in the UK. I was working as a social media editor at the time, which was the "lowest level" staff member in the marketing team, based on the corporate hierarchy system; and because social media was not necessarily seen that important for a business as it is now days. I was however grateful for the opportunity and I enjoyed what I was doing. I was able to use my creativity and communication skills; I had to brainstorm and launch different campaigns and work with influencers and journalists, which I really enjoyed. As I was new in the country, I considered myself so lucky to be there, in an entrepreneurial company, adding value to their overall business results. I never really fitted in the corporate world.

Maybe I was too outspoken for those kinds of organizations and I was definitely not one to be put in a box, it just felt limiting to me. My colleagues were friendly enough and the company CEO and MD were both very nice.

I guess I was doing my job well enough, because not long after starting, I was promoted to a senior role which meant that I was growing both in skill and responsibility, and of course this came with a nice pay rise. I have to admit, being alone in a strange country made me motivated to earn more money, because for the first time in my life, I felt like it would give me the security I needed. This promotion also gave my ego a big boost and I was even more driven to succeed. At that point in my life, I regarded success as an external achievement, the better I was doing, the more successful I felt. A few months into the role however, I found myself day dreaming about wanting more.

There I was a somewhat new face in the company, promoted to a senior role quickly and that just didn't seem to satisfy me enough. This is the problem with external gains, the more you get the more you want. You forget about what once motivated you and you can become so trapped into chasing a social status that it takes over everything else, putting passion and your authentic needs aside. And ultimately, you may find yourself one day with all the things you thought you wanted but still feel they are not enough. The difference between the ego receiving what it wants and the soul being aligned with your actions is a fine line of recognizing what you actually require in order to comply with your authentic self. Of course, back then, I was simply overtaken by satisfying my ego and the more I did so, the more I dug myself a whole of confusion which was to bring me a wake-up call later on in my life.

I had great leaders around me who absolutely led by example, so I became more fascinated with the idea of becoming one of them. I thought to myself, what better way to feel even more successful than to become a manager? My academic background gave me the insight into leadership by understanding the psychology behind behaviour, and I was really inspired to one day become a leader myself, to empower others to use their strengths and achieve big goals. Lucky for me, the amazing managers I had, Abi and Lynsey took me under their wings and became my mentors, later on one of them being the company founder and CEO.

Their success and ability to create results was so interesting to me that I would often watch and observe the ways in which they did their job. I studied the way they spoke and their mannerism. On the rare occasions of me attending some of the higher ups management meetings, I would observe the way they would come up with solutions and what sort of topics they spoke about. I knew that if I wanted to be in the same position I had to commit to working harder than what I was currently putting in. My experience was nowhere near as elevated as theirs, but I was determined to find a way for me to fast track this.

The idea of growing and leading an entire marketing department seemed more exciting to me. One day, we were told that our current marketing manager had suddenly left the company and that meant the role was open for grabs. I had two choices: wait for the moment when one day all my other colleagues who had more experience than me were offered the role and declined/move on from the company or to take responsibility, step up my game and create the reality I wanted to be a part of. My whole life I have been pushing for what I wanted and somehow managed to make it happen, and there was nothing stopping me on this occasion. Of course, I chose the second option because I am a highly competitive individual and I thrive on pushing through challenges especially when it comes to adding value towards my development. When the ego gets continuously satisfied, we tend to be on chase mode constantly.

In that moment, I decided that role was mine and now I had to map out the steps to make it happen. I learned that I had to start putting in double the amount of work I was doing at the time and do more than what my colleagues were doing. I wanted it so badly that I decided to focus solely on it. This meant doing late nights, putting my hand up for the dreaded jobs nobody wanted to do, taking on extra projects. I also knew that I had to make myself and my work noticed and there was only one way to do this and that was through quality and consistency. I made the conscious decision to make sure everything I did was the best work I could do, and that it happened on a consistent basis.

I started learning different processes online, like signing up to free webinars and reading online platforms that are always the first to bring the latest news in the marketing and tech field, such as Mashable and TechCrunch.

I began reading biographies of great entrepreneurs and leaders who achieved greatness in their professional field. I found myself inspired by their words and getting an insight into their successes and failures somehow helped me understand the importance of hardship. Each one of them had a unique story and they all came from different backgrounds and circumstances, but one of the traits they shared in common was accountability. They knew that to make it to the top, they were the ones responsible to make it happen and that meant becoming accountable for their actions.

I became obsessed with the idea of leadership and began watching inspirational YouTube videos from great geniuses like Steve Jobs, Jack Ma and Oprah amongst many others. In doing so, I started to feel even more empowered. I began engaging in conversations with the management team at the company I was working for and discussing the topics they enjoyed. I stopped going to the Friday night after work drinks because I didn't consider this professional for myself and not much fun, especially if I were going to become part of the management team which in my head was already happening.

My vision was clear and I knew my outcome. And through all of this, I started acting like I was already in my desired role. Soon enough, I became the go to person for all marketing queries. The team members were asking me questions and sort of reporting into me; for example, if one of them would call in sick, they would ask for me. If they needed to get annual leave approved, I would be the one they'd send the form to. All of this was happening naturally, without me actually officially getting the manager role, but for me it felt as though I already did and because I started to act like it, everything fell into place organically and even transmitted externally to the others. When you start living in the moment for what you are striving for and begin to act like you have it already, a powerful wave of energy is released in the environment you are in and others around you can pick up on this. We can all feel other people's energies; we might not consciously be aware of it, but at a soul level, this is how we connect.

The only thing I did different was that I started to take responsibility and became accountable for my actions. If I wanted to succeed, I had to be the one who makes it happen. It's just as simple as that. And although I wasn't in control of being given the promotion, what I was responsible for was making sure I did everything I needed in order to fill that role. And I did this by learning, improving my work, my knowledge, my skills and myself on an overall, general level. Most importantly, what made it all come to light was the fact that I saw the big the picture, I felt strongly that I was the ideal candidate for the role, I believed in myself and I was living it. I was now becoming the person in that picture I created for myself. The company CEO, Rob would ask me to report to him weekly about the team's performance. During the monthly company meetings, he would ask me to speak in front of everybody on behalf of the department about the activities we were doing. I was even voted to be the person in charge of the social hub, a committee of ten people in the company who decided on all company events and internal communications. I loved organizing events and I thought this would be a great opportunity for me to become even more involved in the company. Although I was never actually given the job change as a manager, to me it was more important to become a manager by action instead of on paper. I was content enough with my current salary and my desire to step up and be the manager had nothing to do with more income and everything to do with the gained experience that came with it.

I had successfully achieved this and it felt good. Six months later, I decided to leave the company for reasons you will find out about later on in this book. When I handed in my resignation to Rob, he wanted me to stay but was pleased about what was to come next for me. One of the directors even told me that if I stayed, I would have been made the manager. I appreciated his kindness, but I had already accomplished the duties of the role successfully, and most importantly I had proven to myself that I could be whoever and whatever I wanted to be if I take the full responsibility towards it.

Even if I had decided to stay and be given the role, to me it made no difference because that was just a label. The way I saw it is that I was already the marketing manager and the only thing that was missing was the pay rise and the title, which didn't interest me at all. Leaving that company was one of the hardest decisions I faced in my life up until that point, but I listened to my gut and it was time for me to move on. One of the most important aspects of achieving something you truly want is that you have to own your goals and make them become part of your everyday lifestyle. Plato said that we are the actors and the world is our stage and what a wise soul he was. On the surface, we are all performers and the environments we find ourselves in are the platforms we can practice the experiences that we choose to be a part of, the ones we create.

Whatever aspirations you may have and whatever it is that you want to do with your life; you have to know that taking responsibility changes everything. To become the leading character in your life you have to be the one who steps up to the plate. Are you 100% in control of what it is that you want and by taking action, will you definitely achieve your desired outcome? Is there anything else that your goals depend on? Is there somebody else involved in the outcome of the goals? Because in order to achieve anything in your life, you must be the one responsible for making it happen.

Only then you can create the life you would love to live, in the environment you want to be part of, as the leading role you want to take on. After all, it's your life and you deserve to take the spotlight for it.

THE BLAME GAME

When you start to understand the importance of being accountable for your own actions, you will see that pointing fingers at others will not get you anywhere; what you are really doing is pointing towards yourself. When things don't go according to plan, it's easy to blame others, or find different external situations to throw the blame on. The worst approach one can make is to find a self-made explanation about an external reference for everything that goes wrong in their life. Don't you get it? This is your life and you play the leading role in it. There is no director there to guide you and give you the script, you have the freedom to write your own. To make it clearer, you have to learn what it is that you want and then the action plan will follow.

Whatever you decide should be part of your story, when you start taking control and become responsible for your behaviour, you will reach the heights you are aiming towards. Your story will then start to unfold naturally. Whatever experiences you have gone through so far, understand that blaming others will not bring you peace and will definitely not help you move onwards and continue with your story. Sometimes we don't get the closure we want because we chase to find it in the wrong places. Once again, we forget to lead from within and the ego takes the front row. The only way you will find peace is to look internally and search for your own closure. When you start taking control of your life by listening to your intuition and trusting this guidance from within, closure will not even be needed. Once you realize that you must find your inner power, you will become a force living with complete authenticity. It's difficult and sometimes daunting to look inside and discover sides of yourself you never knew you had that are perhaps not as nice as you'd want them to be. It's hard not to get the answers you require from somebody who has decided to break up with you, or not give you that promotion. It's terrifying to look at a situation and accept that maybe you were wrong because the ego will do anything it can to go in self-defence mode. All of these are hard because it means you will have to take ownership and deal with whatever needs to be dealt with so that you can move on and grow.

This is necessary and life was not created to be an easy ride. To do great things, you must start by looking at yourself completely inside and out. Everything begins here. Start with the end. When you look at yourself in the mirror and you don't like what you see, there is an easy way to deal with it or you can simply acknowledge the truth. You can put on some make up and cover what you believe to be flaws, but you can't do that for your internal self, the most authentic part of you. When you don't like something about your life step outside of the box you find yourself stuck in and find a solution. Maybe your life is already filled with all the things you desired, but you are failing to see all of this because of the protective mask you have chosen to wear. If you don't have what you want, dissociate yourself from your thoughts and see the real reason why you want that specific thing. If that aligns with your soul's mission, which will be affirmed by your intuition, you can then start working on your mindset and towards creating processes that will lead to the gains you want. There is nobody else responsible for your life, apart from yourself. The universe will always be there to guide you but if you go against your true self and continue to ignore the messages it gives you, you will just make it harder for yourself. You write your own story. you hold the pen and if you are courageous enough to start look within more, you will be on your way to find the key that unlocks your purpose. It's already inside of you; the challenge of course is to dig deep enough to reach to it.

I am a big believer that the universe will always play an important part in the guidance towards making the right decisions. There is no use on waiting for something to just happen because it won't. The universe will only work together with you when you decide you are open to it. To do so, you need to open you heart and trust its mission for you.

On your life path you will always have a choice to turn around but if you want to truly experience life and succeed at all you want to by staying true to yourself, getting lost on the side streets might actually bring about some exciting possibilities. And if you keep on going, eventually you will be so far away from where you first started that you'll no longer feel familiar with it; but closer to where you should be.

EMBRACE FAILURE

Mr Rob Hill was the name of my first mentor. A successful, award winning entrepreneur with a fast-growing company, Rob was a kind and humble man. Although the founder and CEO of the company I was working for, Rob always led by example. He was the first person to arrive in the office every morning and was always the last one to leave at the end of the day. Rob only took Wednesdays off, but he was there on most other days. His ever-lasting passion for what he did expanded throughout the whole company and many, like myself felt inspired by him. This was never something he was proud of because for Rob what he did was simply what he loved doing and he never considered himself a guru in the business field or an inspirational person, he just did what he was naturally good at.

Rob was featured in many magazines for his great business success and praised about the great culture he managed to create within his own company, something I can definitely agree with having been part of it. There were a lot of travel opportunities available to the staff and we had the best Christmas parties of all. Rob knew how to bring up the morale in the building and he was always positive and encouraging. In my almost three years with the company, I have never once seen Rob angry or shout at somebody. A true born leader, Rob always made sure the highest performers of the company were mentioned in the monthly staff meeting and were given a trophy from the man himself, although he never belittled those who needed an extra push. He was kind and extremely focused on making sure his staff were treated fairly and were given the best encouragement to succeed in whatever they were doing. Amongst the different responsibilities within my role, one of them was doing the public relations for the company and that meant that I was in charge of all the publicity. Rob had a great business story, from humble beginnings to building a successful business that was known not only in the UK but also in other parts of the world. Part of my role was to interview Rob for each article I would write about him and the company before that was published in different magazines and newspapers.

This was my favourite aspect about working there because I always learnt so much from him, a person I looked up to who has successfully managed to reach victory in doing what he loved. It is during those times I became familiar with failure and its importance not only in business, but also in life overall. Until then, I had no idea how much personal and professional hardship and failure a business owner encounters. Rob used to share with me all about the failures he had gone through and how he pushed through these and overcame all obstacles. I learnt all about the difficult times in an entrepreneur's journey and the perseverance that is required to get back on track. I used to sit there and listen to him, completely intrigued and as weird as it sounds, I was eager to one day experience some failures myself because I learnt from him that with these follows success. They balance each other out he used to tell me, and when you fall, get back up and continue following your vision, because you will elevate to a higher level.

I learnt that only when you fail, you will start to appreciate success. I learnt not to fear failure and instead embrace it because with it comes a sense of courage. To this day, I am most grateful to Rob for all the lessons he taught me and most importantly for the time he gave me. A busy businessman, Rob always made sure his office door was open to anybody who wanted to speak with him, and I always took on the opportunity. He was and will forever be my first mentor, the man who showed me the reality behind being an entrepreneur and the person who helped me realize I can do much more than what I was doing back then.

He believed and saw something in me I myself could not at the time. He saw my hunger and potential and encouraged me to always follow my heart and do something that I loved because only then I would be able to truly enjoy it and stay true to myself. Rob helped re-evaluate my capabilities and the skills and talent I had for what I was doing. I will always have tremendous respect for him.

We all want to be successful but the price we pay for success can be much higher than what we expected to bargain for. Success is not something that gets handed to us on a silver platter, but in most cases, it is quite the opposite. Behind all the great victories, there is a story of hardship and maybe even some darkness. Some people look at high achievers and think "This person is so lucky, I wish I could do that". What Rob taught me is that anything is possible but are you prepared to do all that it takes to make it happen? No matter what you want to do, know that there will be moments when you will fall. Sometimes, you will keep failing, but this I have learnt is a sign that success is to follow and it is in these moments that we are tested about how badly we really want it. Success is not so much about the outcomes as it is about the steps you take to get there. It is during these moments that we discover the mystery of the journey and how dynamic it can be.

What separates successful people from the rest is that they actually make things happen by taking risks, by believing in themselves and their vision and continuing to do so regardless how many times they fail. To them, there are no problems or roadblocks, only solutions. Their passion and desire to succeed is simply something they are not willing to compromise. When you stay true to yourself and do something that aligns with your soul's mission, no number of spikes along the way will stop you. Because there is a reassurance from within that's so strong it helps you to keep going. Failure can be a daunting word for most of us and we often see it as a negative experience, but what we continue to ignore is that failure can actually push us much further than we think into a land of unlimited possibilities.

If you understand this, you will realize that failures are supposed to come your way, because only then you will recognize and truly savour your success. If whatever it is that you want is important enough to you, failure will force you to tap into your most powerful resources and use them wisely. Your creativity will blossom by using your imagination; you will become more solution driven by using your mind to its full potential; and you will see the worth of going through the struggles when you are passionate about what you want and feel it from your core.

Nobody is perfect, we are human beings and there is no special book to teach us how to live. It comes naturally and mistakes are all part of the plan. The biggest mistakes I've made so far in my life were the most eye-opening experiences I have gone through. Looking back to these I realized that I needed a wake-up call or a complete shift in my thinking in order to go towards my true purpose. Whenever I look back at the toughest moments of my life, I can't help but feel some sense of satisfaction. Whether I realized it at the time or not, those moments where I saw nothing but darkness, were actually the ones that shed the most light on my path later on.

The universe is beautiful and it's always on your side if you let it. When you fail at something, your first instinct is to beat yourself up for it. You will feel like a failure and think that you are not good enough to do whatever it is that you want to achieve. When failure occurs, your ego comes out stronger. Its influence on you will be more powerful because all it wants to do is keep you "safe" by not acknowledging that you failed but that you can keep going. It always knows when to come to your "rescue" but comfort will never bring you growth. Use your ego as a reason to push even harder. When that little voice prompts you to give up because it's too risky or too hard, prove it wrong and know you can do it by following your intuition. Knowing your worth has more to do with the way you interpret your personal power from within and how you utilize your intuition, and never with the way others perceive you to be.

Never fear about what others might think of you if you fail, they will think whatever they want regardless. You cannot aim to please everybody but one person in this whole world and that is YOU. If you can focus on this, you are already a winner for yourself. You will never know just how amazing you are at something until you give it a try. You might fail the first time, second and third, even a tenth time, but if you keep going, knowing deep down that it is what you are meant to be doing, it will no doubt happen for you. Patience and perseverance, the two magic words I try to live my life by, really work every time.

Know that everything that happens is an experience you are meant to be going through and that its intention is to lead you to your next chapter in life, closer to your life's purpose. Sometimes we can't explain it, and often there is no need to question it. Just know that what you want you can have so long as it is aligned with your soul's purpose. Make friends with failure, embrace it, learn from it and get better at accepting it.

SIX

COMMITMENT

Habits are created by repeating the same behaviours on a consistent basis until they get recognized by our subconscious mind and then we do them automatically. The more you do something; the more it will become part of your routine. Like a computer, the human brain records everything and has a limitless capacity of receiving and storing information. With the mind however you don't have an erase history button and even though your cognitive information may get lost somewhere in the back of your mind, it is still there.

The most amazing thing is that you can access this information any time and you can use previous life lessons learnt to aid you towards a better outcome in the present. Everybody has the power and ability to be disciplined. In the *Collins dictionary, discipline is described as "the practice of making people obey rules or standards of behaviour and punishing them when they do not". To me, discipline is a process in which one makes the conscious decision to stick to a specific behaviour in order to implement consistency within their life. We can have a disciplined mind by deciding what we want to think about more and what we choose to eliminate from our thoughts. When you practice everything with integrity, you remain true to yourself. You will know this is happening, when what you do becomes a primary focus that is driven from within with love and kindness, and not motivated by external factors, situations or negative feelings. If you follow your intuition and listen to your internal guidance, discipline and commitment are easier to be maintained. There is no greater force than the one, which comes from our soul. When you feel your true calling, nothing can stop you from going for it unless you create your own limitations. Discipline is vital because it teaches us to focus and be patient. We might not see the results for a long time; but one who finds the discipline to continue in pursuing their truth, will no doubt live with more genuine intention and remain truthful to their original self. I've always been driven to learn more. Although I hardly enjoyed going to school, what I did love is learning.

Leonardo Da Vinci once wrote that "Learning never exhausts the mind" and in fact I feel exhausted if I don't continue to learn. Of course, I wasn't passionate about all the subjects I did in school, but I was always open to learning about each one. The brain is like a muscle and it develops further the more information we give it. Through learning, not only do we gain more information about areas we didn't know of before, but it also introduces us to discipline.

Regardless of what your IQ is, without finding the discipline to commit to continuous learning, you will not be able to open yourself to more information. I have challenged myself to constantly be open to learning and take new courses all the time. Even after my psychology degree and holistic medicine diplomas, I remain interested to dig even deeper. I am a huge believer in the importance of constantly gaining more knowledge and the more you learn, the more you expand the potential your mind can offer you. The first time I was promoted to the senior executive role in the UK I was pleased with myself. I worked hard to make that happen and the results followed. My role included more responsibility and even more hard work. I had never been a 9-5 kind of professional anyway, because to me this is simply the average amount required. I detest the word average and all my life I strived and continue to go beyond what is considered average, or at least what I perceive to be average. Mediocrity never agreed with me or I with it.

The thought of falling into a routine that will soon become monotonous is not what I aspire to and this has always been a barrier I had pushed through. I worked hard and was committed to providing consistent results within my job and in following this came the promotion. I truly enjoyed my new role and made the most of it, but I wanted to learn more about something else, I was interested in colouring my life with new knowledge. I sensed an urge to add to my self-development and gain an additional qualification to my academic achievements I had so far.

Neuro linguistic programming had been an interest of mine since I first heard about it. Growing up, I admired Tony Robbins for his bravery and his splendid public speaking skills. I wanted one day to be on stage just like him and empower people, thousands and thousands of them. So, I enrolled in an online, home study NLP course that had the deadline of completion in a year's time. It was April 2015 and driven to make things happen, I set myself up the goal of completing it by the 28th of July 2015, which is my birthday. As I began studying, I realized just how unrealistic my deadline seemed. The modules were long and required a lot of reading, writing, analyzing, and it even had practical components as well. I discovered that in order to make the deadline I set myself up for, I had to create a system and commit to it.

I became extremely disciplined in my approach and divided my time wisely. My system was simple and achievable. Every evening after work I would go to the gym and afterwards I would go home and have dinner. I enjoy cooking so I devoted at least one hour to cooking, eating and cleaning up. Once this was done, I would commit to a minimum of 3 hours every night for my studies, which would end just before midnight. During the weekends, I would spend five hours or so studying and completing the assignments.

I realize this sounds very robotic, and when I look back, it really was in a way. But discipline is always required to achieve your goals. I confess though that it wasn't easy to do. I was tired and sometimes, I would finish my dinner and would just want to spend time with my friends. But then I would snap out of it by reminding myself that in doing so, I wouldn't reach my desired results. So, I'd grab my books and start. I kept focused on the end result and I was taking the steps required to reach it. Two months later and 30 days before my deadline, I sent through my final assignment and received my NLP Practitioner certificate. By becoming focused, disciplined and committed to the structure I created for myself, I was able to achieve my goal. It was difficult and sometimes I dreaded the thought of it all, but I remained committed throughout the entire process and with every new chapter I'd learn about, I'd become even more driven because I knew that I was getting closer to the finish line. Little by little, day-by-day, I had reached my desired results.

Without committing yourself to your goals, you will very rarely be able to achieve much. Consistency is one of the most valuable characteristics for success, and with this comes discipline. Although it can appear to be restrictive at times, setting up a structured plan to identify and execute the steps required is extremely important. Regardless of how driven you are and how often you visualize your desired success, if you don't commit to consistent action towards your goals, they will simply remain dreams and images in your mind.

One of my favourite *quotes says, "Don't die with the music still inside you" and without manifesting this on the physical dimension, your music will never be heard. The spiritual self sends guidance, but the physical part of our self is the one that puts it in motion and manifests it. The two always have to be connected. Everybody has a unique way of doing things and you are responsible for finding yours. The strategic plan you create will be the foundation you need to get started, so find a system that works for you but one that will also challenge you. If it is too easy to achieve, turn it up a notch because if it's not challenging, you will soon become distracted and lose focus. Assess why your goal is so important to you and find the intentions that will push you towards it. And when this importance becomes a must for you, then you will no doubt find the discipline required. Your life is what you make of it and it should be filled with events that you choose to represent your reality.

When you start to realize this, you will become committed to everything that you want to manifest for yourself. Too many people get lost in the lives of others' and without being aware, they let themselves far too influenced by these external factors. We tend to look at what others have and feel as though what we have is not good enough, even if we have everything we want. It is the ego that brings out this behaviour not to confuse us, but in its own protective way, to push us to chase for even more.

But there is only so much you can chase, before you realize that not everything is really as it seems. We look at the realities of others and fail to focus and be grateful for our own. What matters is how you feel about your life and what actions you will take to become one with your true self. Commit to this type of thinking. Start writing ideas down, practice visualization daily, say your affirmations and commit to doing so. Instead of relying on others or external situations to make things happen for you, start relying on yourself to do so. Make it your number one mission to commit to every action that will create the reaction you desire.

PERSEVERANCE

Everybody in this world has experienced negative thinking at some point. For some people, it happens more often than for others. When you look at your thoughts for exactly what they are, you can then start to be selective about what you are actually thinking about. You might not believe that you can have control of your thoughts, and perhaps that is true in that moment. The mind is a complex system and sometimes it can trick us into not using it to its full ability. Our thoughts can have tremendous power over our life and can shape our realities. When I left my final year of high school, I was accepted into a fashion course with AUT University. I was 17 years old and my creativity was at an all-time high. I loved clothes and I loved the idea of designing. I never read many books until I reached my early 20's but I can say I owned every Vogue issue from the age of 15. For a teenager at that time, to buy Vogue magazine every month was an absolute treat. It was expensive, but completely worth it. I would sit for hours and browse through each issue, being swept away on an endless wave of inspiration from seeing such beautiful designs and reading about the great artists and creative minds who were behind the trends to come. After reading each issue over and over again, I would start doing magazine cut outs and create my monthly inspiration mood board, which covered the walls in my room for most of my teenage years. I thought because I was so passionate about it that it must've been what I was meant to be doing with my life. I enjoyed studying at AUT. The tutors were extremely skilled and I had made some really good friends. University life suited me much better than school, because we were actually given the freedom to be creative and use our imagination.

Around half way through my first year, I began wondering about how I could actually gain some work experience. I am a fan of learning indeed, but I thought practical experience was more suited for me in the fashion industry. Besides, I didn't really want to sit lectures for three more years to learn about being creative or about the history of fashion. I had been doing so with all those Vogue issues since I was 15. I also wanted to be part of the fashion world, to mix and mingle with the designers and attend the fashion shows. One day I decided to approach one of my university professors and discuss with her my opportunities for gaining some work experience with some real-life designers. She explained to me that the industry was very competitive especially in a small country like New Zealand, with a population of just under 5 million people. She advised me to continue with my bachelors' degree for another three years and surely after that I would be skilled enough to pursue the field myself. I wasn't a rebellious type of student, but I couldn't really relate to what she was saying. I was young, passionate about the field, somewhat talented and had lots of energy, why would I spend three more years in a building with professors, when I could be spending my time in an atelier with successful fashion designers learning by doing? The truth is I had itchy feet and I simply couldn't see myself there for much longer. Determined to show her that it is possible, I started emailing all the fashion designers in the city I was in to ask for work. Things didn't prove to be that easy, especially when most of the emails I received back were rejections.

But I wasn't going to give up. I knew that this was my solution and all I needed was one yes, just one. After a few weeks had gone by, I decided to send another email to all the designers who rejected me. I was clearly a bit of a fearless soul, but my intuition guided me to be perseverant. I wasn't at all concerned with what they would think of me trying again, because I just wanted the work. I thought that if I email them again, at least one of them would see just how hungry I was for it. To my surprise, after a few more months of rejection emails, one day I got my yes. When that email came through, I was so excited I read it over and over again. I had put my intention out there and the universe had given me even more than I expected. I was actually offered a paid role being the second personal assistant to an amazing New Zealand fashion designer, who is now days even more successful and I am incredibly pleased to see. Once I completed my first year at AUT, I left with a job offer and I made sure to let that one professor know, the one who told me it will not be possible. Maybe this had showed her that sometimes it's ok to encourage students to go beyond what they think is possible. In September, when fashion week came, I was actually working behind the scenes and getting paid for it whilst my old colleagues were doing full days of experience, unpaid.

What I learned in that moment when my yes came is that no matter how many doors keep closing on you, one day the right door will definitely open. And the only way to make this happen is to go and find that key; to create a solution that will get you closer to your goal. I never once doubted myself, even when I kept receiving emails that said no. I just kept going because I knew that I would eventually get what I had hoped for, I believed in it too much for it not to happen. I was extremely confident about my abilities and although some saw it as arrogance, I thought otherwise. It is important that you are confident with yourself and your ability to win through challenges. There is nothing really stopping you but yourself. It is you who decides what your limits are and how far along the barriers you want to keep pushing. You have endless opportunities and it is your choice whether you take them or not; but first you must see them. Whatever you tell yourself and how often you do it, determines what results you are getting. Whether it is limiting beliefs that have stopped you until now, or the fear of failure, know that these are both part of the process Without fear, you will never really understand just how courageous you are. Learn from your self-limiting beliefs and test them out to see if they are actually real or if you are just creating them based on your fears. The true character of a person is revealed when they keep tripping over, but still persevere to make it to the finish line. The more you practice by challenging your fear, the further you will continue to grow. Living on the surface for the sakes of just surviving is comforting but not elevating. You will never really feel truly alive until you start using all you have been given in order to manifest and create what you are here to do.

Let your mind, imagination and passion guide you and know that nobody can take these away from you. People may reject you, they might even put you down, judge you or even ignore you, but the actions you take for yourself are what matter and will be the ones that empower you to keep going.

SEVEN

WORK FOR IT

All the successful people I came across so far in my life told me that hard work and commitment were the two key factors that got them to reach their triumphs. And although these were their resources to get them there, they were able to maintain it because they listened to the voice within, and by taking big risks they got to their truth. I truly believe there is no special formula for success; you just have to work hard for what you want but first you must identify what that is. There is little to be said about those who inherit great fortunes and chose to remain oblivious to reaching their potential because if you don't have to work for it, what is truly the meaning of it? Without the blood, sweat and tears behind it, everything is simply just a puppet show you put on for others in which you somehow fall in the illusion that you've earned it.

How are you meant to discover yourself and all the greatness you are capable of, if there are no challenges and no quests for you to embark on? My grandmother was poor for most of her life. As a little girl, I remember the joy I'd feel when I was to spend the night at her place, a tiny apartment on the seventh floor. I would spend time on her balcony trying to conquer my fear of heights, but always greatly failed at this because I could not get myself to walk further than the glass door separating the room from the balcony. I think this phobia of mine actually started whilst spending time there, because it was the first time I was exposed to being so high up in a building and somehow, I could never get myself to understand the concept that although it was very far from the ground, I would still be able to feel stable. My grandmother was the most beautiful person I have ever met, inside and out. She was kind, loving and a very wise lady. At times, she would have as little as three ingredients in her pantry, but the magic she would create with those astonished me. She'd make the best cakes, read me the best bed time stories and taught me a great wealth of knowledge.

To her, wealth was something she possessed as a human being from within. An opera singer, speaker of three languages, self-taught and the best dressed lady I have ever seen, she lived her life with more prosperity than any other financially wealthy person I knew. She taught me that people don't need to know how much money you have, you just need to be the best version of yourself you approve of.

She'd say that if you respected yourself enough to look after your looks and what you did have, nobody will ever know how or wonder how much money you have because they wouldn't care. People are stuck in the illusion of seeing materialistic things as a modality to measure one's wealth. But the secret is in how you interpret the true meaning of it. If you consider yourself wealthy by using all that you have, you won't miss out on life's greatest pleasures and that is living as if you had it all.

When I was 14 years old and halfway through my first year of high school in New Zealand, I began acting like a true teenager. I discovered the world of shopping and decided I needed new clothes and make up. One day, my mother sat down with me and opened a discussion around all the new things I was wanting to have. She said I can have the make-up and the clothes and everything else my teenager self was desiring but if I wanted all of this I needed to work for them. In that moment, I realized that it was time for me to get my first job. So, I approached the local takeaway store that just happened to be looking for a counter girl; on the spot, I found out the job was mine.

I wasn't too fond of this because it was the place where everyone at school hangout during the weekends. I was embarrassed to be seen in this place especially because shortly after I began working there my school colleagues knew me as the fish and chips takeaway girl. It wasn't my favourite nickname but on the upside, I was now earning my own money and at 14 I was able to buy all the things that I thought I needed. I was working two evenings after school and both weekend days.

Although I was only supposed to be the counter girl, my eagerness to learn more pushed me to also help out in the kitchen and after 6 months; they gave me a pay rise and asked me if I wanted to be an assistant manager. This may not sound like the dream job for many, but for me at the time it was an accomplishment and my way to become more independent and responsible from that young age. It was during this period I discovered the concept that if you work hard, you will excel in whatever it is you desire. Through hard work, more knowledge is acquired and a whole new self can be born just by being curious to learn more.

My first year of high school was tough. I was struggling to juggle it all with a complete culture shock including a new language. A 14-year-old with lots of ambition but no friends was not good enough for me. Once again, I was failing to fit in but my motivation was stronger than ever. So, I decided to befriend people who were considered the "geeks" of the school. They were the only ones who actually talked to me at that point and that was ok with me. I decided to focus more on my studies than I did trying to impress my colleagues. With English, not being my first language I had to work very hard on my studies. My love for writing and poetry pushed me to perfect my writing and grammatical skills in the language and by the end of my first year of high school I became the top student in my English class.

I was also part of the debate team and I even made it into the school choir which I never understood how because I can't sing very well at all. But I made it because I wanted to prove myself that anything is possible. It's funny how when you believe you can do something, others start to believe in you also. My English teacher enjoyed my writing and was probably as surprised as I was that I could write so well in a new language I had only properly learnt that year. How did I do it? I worked so hard at mastering my craft and was not going to accept anything less.

That's the thing about hard work. When you focus your mind on a particular outcome and you know what you are working towards and continue to push through whatever obstacles come your way, no doubt you will shine because you will figure out the steps you need to take to get there. There is quite a strong correlation between working hard and working smart. When you know what you are working towards and focus solely on that, you will make it happen. You have to decide how important the outcome really is to you. When you set your intention towards it and you decide that nothing will stop you; then nothing will. Working hard is more than just doing the average required.

You must put in more hours than perhaps you'd like; you will probably need to give up other activities that take up your time and you enjoy doing; you will have to think outside of your comfort zone and push yourself to greater heights and most importantly, you have to believe you can do it. My mother has been a great example for me growing up. A great mother, loving wife, successful journalist now turned business owner, I grew up seeing her work all the time. If she needed to get two jobs, she did just that. Her outcome was to be able to give my brother and I everything we needed and she was determined to do it no matter what. And that's why she always succeeded.

When you give it all you have you will soon realize that you have even more to give. You will encounter challenges. You will feel tired, exhausted, worn out, perhaps you will feel stressed, embarrassed, confused and you might even start doubting yourself. As soon as you push yourself outside of your comfort zone, your ego will come and remind you of it so that it can create some fear in order for you to get back in your comfort zone. It doesn't like to take risks because it fears the unknown and with its intention to protect, it actually will try to scare you away from what it is you aspire to do. The trick here is to not give in to that, but to keep on going forwards by reminding yourself why you started, therefore of your intention. Most people will start giving up as soon as the ego comes into play. It will help them rationalize somehow that all of this is simply not worth it because of the pressure it brings.

You might start comparing yourself to others and say, "Well I'm never going to get to that level", or "I've given it my all already and nothing came out of it" or "I've had enough of this". And this is ok, but if you have set your mind to great big things, these are simply excuses and challenges you are meant to overcome. You can get to that level, you certainly will always have more to give and it is all about what you want and how you choose to go get it. Your perception of how life should be as simply that, your own view. One entrepreneur I worked with described his constant pushing through challenges and the sleepless nights as tranquil because for him that's what peace meant: doing what he loved and doing it well no matter what came with it. Tranquillity often comes from the most turbulent of times and you must know that you are equipped enough to handle all that comes your way. It is simply how you choose to interpret something that will lead you to your next step. Challenges will almost always unlock opportunities and opportunities will always come with challenges. This is how balance is created and we must find this equilibrium to understand its significance in our life.

CHALLENGES

My determination to "make it" has been so important all my life that nothing would ever be able to get in the way of this. In fact, I used one of the most tragic events in my life to push me towards breaking boundaries even further. Pain quickly vanished into motivation for me and I never looked back. When my father left, my life was all of a sudden turned upside down. I never really understood the meaning of loss until this event came into my life. My best friend for 20 something years one day chose to depart as quickly as the memories we created faded. The truth is, I never thought my parents were destined for one another and although I should've been happy that the arguing finally stopped, I was in despair. Until then, my family was my anchor. Every time I was in need of comfort I would spend time with them. Their love made me feel accepted and safe and we were a family unit, so that somehow made me feel like I belong. But as I was starting to notice, things are not always as they seem to be as sometimes we are distracted by our own desire to see an image as we would hope it to be and not for the actual truth it holds. After 30 something years of marriage, they finally called it quits by him one day leaving with my mum's best friend who was a very wealthy lady. They have been seeing each other in secret, an affair that lasted some odd years before they finally spoke their truth.

I never really understood how he was able to succeed in his mysterious plan of constant cheating and still be the one who decides, but later on I realized this was a blessing from the universe. My father was a man with little drive and not much passion either. His only interest was monetary value, he loved having things and bragging about them. Of course, growing up I saw him as a role model because we were very close. He used to take me to volleyball practice and help me get my spike stronger because in his younger days he played the sport as well.

He often helped me with my failed attempts to pass math in school, which to this day I have no idea how I managed to do so. And he used to make me laugh as a kid, he was funny when he wanted to be. He wasn't a bad father, but the day he chose to leave he also decided to leave my brother and I. His new girlfriend had three children from her previous marriage, and now he was taking them to swimming practice and doing the school drop offs, as I was often told by friends who had seen him do so. Although we lived in the same area but never actually saw him, I felt embarrassed when my friends would tell me about their accidental sight of him. It felt as though they were speaking about a stranger, because I could still not believe the man I grew up seeing as honest and kind, would turn out to be one of the biggest disappointment lessons I had to learn.

I suppose the emotional benefits from having a loving family were never enough for him; he wanted money and lots of it. In a way I don't blame him, we were poor for most of our life so why would he want to continue through it? He saw his opportunity with this new lady, who pretended to be a family friend, all whilst she was having an affair with my father. She had money and to me she was not very bright, which meant that my father was able to play her and my mother at the same time, who unlike the mistress, was intelligent but blinded by a naiveté of being in love, or whatever she would call it. When your love for the people around you is not enough, your ego will convince you to seek more somewhere else because if you cannot love those around you, the love you give to yourself is lacking. But what I realized is that perhaps is not so much the external love but instead the internal comfort of your own self that you project out there in the world, for those around you. After it happened, and after my anxious aftermath, came something quite magical. I decided that I needed to shift my mindset and started to take it as an opportunity to create a change in my life and embark on a new chapter, stronger and more empowered. I used every single bit of anger and resentment I had within me towards him and changed it for motivation. I was sick of giving my power to the unfortunate events that had occurred, and instead I focused on my internal state and how I could create more structure in my life to achieve the things I wanted and knew I was worthy of.

This abrupt ending also brought my brother and I closer. Before the official break-up between my parents, we both assisted plenty of our parents' horrific arguments. Screaming, shouting, cursing, hurtful words…we were both there experiencing it all and I think this made us realize how glad we are to have each another. My older brother, unlike my father is a man of his word. Strong willed, passionate, talented and intelligent, Amos and I started to get along really well. Not that we didn't before, after all we grew up together. I was the annoying, rebellious little sister, but he always looked out for me. We were very different growing up. He was friendly, extremely tidy and popular, and I was curiously questioning everything, enjoyed my own space, quite messy and not very popular.

But now, there was a sense of deeper understanding for one another and we both decided to make an effort to stay in touch and look out for one another. All my life, whilst growing up I admired his ability to do what he wants and be who he is. He was confident, had loads of friends and was a fantastic student at school getting the best grades, everybody loved him. He inspires me in so many ways, and even though sometimes he is brutally honest, he has one of the kindest hearts I know. When in need, I always go to him for advice or a second opinion; he just has this amazing ability to see things as they are, without having to question anything. It's strange how sometimes we need moments of losing somebody to appreciate others who are part of our life.

You will always encounter roadblocks and setbacks within your path. Life is not meant to be a linear journey, for if it were, we'd all become a bunch of lazy people with no understanding of how much we are truly capable of. Life is as much about the side streets you stumble on as it is about your final destination. In fact, I believe that it is the challenges that help us find the genius within and open the door to spirituality. We are all born with a genius like tendency. For whatever subject or field, you have the ability within you to become a genius of your own craft as long as your passion aligns with it. The mind is both magical and complex so the more you push beyond your limiting beliefs, the more you uncover layers of greatness within you. *Richard Branson, one of the most successful and innovative entrepreneurs of the 21st century once said that "My interest in life comes from setting myself huge, apparently unachievable challenges and trying to rise above them". We tend to look at successful people such as Sir Branson and wonder how they can continuously achieve so much. We consider people like him geniuses and find it hard to relate because they are so far out from the average that we think they must have some special superpowers given at birth. But I am certain that all is possible, and we can all be that genius, we already are but fail to acknowledge this.

Alongside success, there will be failure and lots of it. But failure balances out success, and without it I really don't think success is possible. The more mistakes you make and challenges you endure, the more successful you become so long you continue to take action and learn. With every obstacle or failed attempt, you have a choice. To get back up and continue to try again or give up and go back to point A, where it all began. But don't you see how far you've come already? Aren't you just a little bit curious to take an extra step? Can't you see you have already taken many steps and what you are experiencing now is an aftershock that will soon go away? When you embark on life's greatest adventures you'll need to be patient; because great things take time and it is the sole reason why they are great, for which they come with effort, challenges and many lessons to be learnt.

*"**Many of life's failures are people who did not realize how close they were to success when they gave up.**"*

Thomas Edison.

EIGHT

THE TOWER MOMENT

True happiness is recognizing and appreciating the simplicity of life. Material things lose their value quickly and their meaning vanishes almost instantly once acquired, but the beautiful nature around us, in all its simplicity continues to add worth to our existence. Chasing a social status to prove one's value only feeds the ego, and this leads to a dangerous downward spiral of self-inflicted selfishness. We are therefore led to believe that the true meaning of life lies within acquiring man made wealth. Becoming distracted by these false desires, we fail to recognize the true purpose we are here to experience. When we are able to put the ego aside together with its desires and feel accomplished and whole without the artificial glamour we feed ourselves with, that awakens our senses, nurtures our soul, heals our wounds and reveals the clarity of living with our most authentic purpose.

After 3 years of living in the UK I decided it was once again time to spread my wings and explore a new destination. The truth is I loved it here; I loved what I was doing and I enjoyed the time spent with the friends I had made. But my gut was telling me there was somewhere new I should be and since the best advice I ever got has always been from my gut, I decided to follow it. Taking big risks has never stopped me and I had already been exposed to the great possibilities that present themselves to me when I make decisions that shake everything up. Just like the tower card in tarot spreads tells us, the foundations we work on are never completely as solid as we think they are, for they can crumble at any moment. Regardless of how strong they may be, the power of the fire explosion often illustrated in the Tower major arcana has caused it to collapse, not so that everything ends, but so that something new can be built again. Sometimes we hold onto ideas about where we should be and what we should be doing that it can be hard to let go of.

And when something of a great force comes and shakes up our strong base that we had worked towards for years and years, we fall in despair. We lose all hope and become confused and lost in our own reality, the one we thought we wanted to be part of, the one we so obviously created for ourselves. Everything in that moment can appear to be a complete blank, we cannot see further than what we have built. But this is because we hold onto the belief that we must be in control of everything that happens for us and instead we fail on just focusing to write our own story.

So, when the time comes for the crash to occur, we need to step back and decide what is to be built next. The beauty of this chaos of course is in the arrival of a new beginning this crash prompts. The universe constantly reminds us of the balance needed to create harmony between our self as the soul and the created self, the illusionary one we make to fit in with the physical world. I knew my tower moment had begun and I myself started to tear the walls down, the ones I have been shaping for the last few years. I was desperate to enter a new phase of my life without being aware of how to actually do this. But I had all the tools available to make this happen and I am grateful for the level of consciousness I was able to gain about this. Through my experiences, I found a new life philosophy in which I became to discover my spiritual side, and this encouraged me to trust in myself and to be brave.

Greatness comes from being aware of the negatives and the positives that can come upon us, and for some reason I was always able to recognize this. Challenges rarely frightened me because I recognized their existence in the meaning of creation. Following through with my decision to return to the Southern Hemisphere, I wasn't interested in living back in New Zealand because I wanted to continue pursuing big things professionally and this was not the place for me to do so. New Zealand has provided me with so much love and many experiences that have sparked my curiosity to seek beyond what I knew even further, so it was a very special place for me. But it is a small country and a place I feel very comfortable in, and yet again I was seeking to go beyond this comfort. I have never been attracted to the big fish in a small pond type ideology, so I wanted to be in a place where I would be challenged; to be surrounded by great souls who would inspire and help me discover more layers about myself aside from those I was already aware of.

I wanted to learn and continue to explore new things, so the next best option would be its neighbouring land, Australia. A country with big cities which came with lots of opportunities and a lot more sunshine than London had to offer. As much as I knew I would miss my family and friends, I had come too far to go back now and being alone again didn't scare me because it meant I was about to learn more lessons and get outside of my comfort zone even more which is when my soul really comes alive.

As I had gained more experience in my career and departing encouraging words of wisdom from my first mentor Rob, I had also found the confidence to know exactly what I wanted and trusted myself that I would be worthy and capable of achieving it. It was all I wanted at the time and I somehow always knew it would eventually manifest itself for me. I saw it in my mind and felt it in my gut, which was already proof of its existence; I just had to find a way to physically make it happen also.

When you are about to embark on a new voyage you will no doubt feel confused and sometimes even scared, but you must always look within and find your truth or at least a small part of it which you can hold onto as a reminder of your intentions. It's there and has always been. No amount of fear or mental chatter can take that away from you. It's printed on your inner walls so strongly that it forever remains, with or without your physical self.

During my first week in Melbourne, the city I decided to move to, I had two job interviews. And just like my previous experience with these, the first one was not suitable nor aligned with my purpose but the second was going to be my golden key to unlocking my purpose even further; because from the moment I stepped into that office, I knew I was meant to be there. Remember the office with the orange wall I once saw in my most powerful meditation? As I walked into the building for the first time, there it was- that big orange wall and it was then I knew my path was meant to cross with this place.

Sometimes life can take us by surprise and fall into place exactly as we imagine it, at the right time in the right space. This happens of course when you have the courage to leave behind any material gains you once created and dive into a new adventure, without having the security of knowing exactly what will come, but instead trusting that there is a greater meaning behind all of it. Through the connection you have with yourself and your soul, you can feel or be prompted about what's to come. You will not be given a full script of everything you will experience on this new course you will take on, but you will be guided, supported and protected if you only trust yourself to do so. When you trust yourself, you awaken a sense of humble confidence that can aid you in any adventures you choose to take on. What is confidence if it's not the sole trust within ourselves and the universe around us? When you are confident, you trust yourself enough to make the right decisions. Self-trust brings love; it brings joy and authentic power. Let your soul guide your truth, for when your mind leads with thoughts of kindness and love, fear diminishes. When you start living as your original self and in confidence of appreciating yourself as a human being both on a physical and spiritual energetic level, the universe will reward you and the doors of infinite possibilities will open themselves for you.

I knew somehow that breaking free from all ties I had restricted myself with would bring me to a place of clarity. Although my ego was revealing ideals of more successes I would reach, I had also become connected with my spiritual side, one that was guiding me toward peace and tranquillity. And as I became aware of these two completely opposing forces, they both played a valuable role in this phase of my life and what was to come. Contrary to my past experiences, I was now mindful of the fact that although I wanted to gain more advancement and prosperity in my life, this would no longer be measured solely by the external rewards my ego was tempting me to reach out for. I was genuinely familiar with the need to grow even further, not to deny the ego but to see what would happen if I let it guide me together with the wiser part of me, the guidance of my soul. I knew the ego holds my fears and that at some moment it will bring these out, however I now felt more equipped than ever to face them.

NINE

RELATIONSHIPS AND HEARTBREAK

It seems almost ironic for me to write about love since I have never really had a serious relationship that lasted more than six months. But what I believe I can elaborate on to a complete deepness is heartbreak. We all experience it in different ways and its meaning to our development is necessary. I am so familiar with this concept and have experienced it enough to create a conclusion upon the miracles that can come from it.

As I look back at my previous intimate relationships, I cannot say they were failed attempts. The truth is, each man who came into my life, for whatever period of time, taught me something which brought value to me. The influence and impact these lessons had upon my self-development sparked a curiosity in me to get closer to the real Miriam, the most original part of me. With every break-up, I felt a sense of heartbreak, but also of hope. Every single one of these men opened their hearts to me at some point in their life and that is a unique experience and one that I express gratitude towards. I may have thought that things did not work out as they should have, but the truth is they did. Everything that happened for me is part of a bigger picture filled with a series of events that I must go through in order to reach that moment of clarity and understanding. Often, we are so caught up in the feeling of loss that we blind ourselves from the truth and with every emotion of sadness and grief, we continue to take steps further away from our own true self. Every life experience is brought to us so that we can learn valuable lessons from which we can expand spiritually. And whilst in that moment we may not see this, as time goes by we can certainly open our heart to feeling this way, not so we could get closure, but so that we could free ourselves from any attachment that our mind or emotional self has tried to cling onto. From the man who cheated on me, I learned the importance of forgiveness and not to repeat his mistakes upon others. From the man who left me to pursue his career and focus on his passions, I learned that I needed to place importance on my dreams and continue to search for the experiences in which I can provide service and bring value to the world.

From the man who was hurt when I ended the relationship, I learned the lesson of compassion and being caring towards other's feelings. From the man who lied to me, I learnt the importance of speaking the truth. And from the man who loved me and me him, but there was a greater force that kept pushing us apart, I learnt to be patient and trust in divine timing. As a collective, through all these relationships, I was inspired to open my heart and believe in true love and that it is all around us. I had opened myself to the possibility that we can genuinely give and receive it at any time, with or without the self-created expectations as an outcome. There is no reason to be cruel in thought against others, simply because a relationship didn't fit our expectations. We all feel differently, and it is our right to do so. We are individuals who all share a similar road but take on different paths and we can go through experiences as we feel it fits our own perception of reality, and most importantly one we can connect with. There are no coincidences, and everything is meant to happen when it does. Anger and resentment will take us further away from the truth, whilst love and kindness will open our eyes to see what we are meant to see and our hearts to feel more than we think we can.

I had to learn the hard way and it seems that the universe wanted me to do so. I am completely sure that the universe and its power is with us every moment of every day. We are spiritually guided and protected in all decisions we make and the experiences that follow from these. The universe always has our back, it's almost as if it lets us take the wheel, but it's still very much in control of what is happening. At any point, it has the power to pull the hand break when it needs to do so. The universe leads the way and we are divinely guided and trusted to take that wheel and go wherever we believe is right for us. Sometimes, of course what we believe is the right way, may not necessarily be it.

We know when we take a wrong turn or make a wrong decision because we feel it. It goes against our soul's desire and we feel this deep down, at our core. But many people will choose to ignore their body's signals and let the ego lead. When this happens, and we find ourselves stuck in a moment when we fall in the despair of "why me", that is the moment when the universe decided to pull that hand break so that we can pause and see things more clearly. Going against our soul's purpose and guidance will no doubt get us caught into a bit of a rut or at least we perceive it to be so.

In love and relationships, I can confidently say the universe pulled many hand breaks for me. I never really dreamt of finding my prince and this has not been a priority of mine at any point in my life. But I admit that at times, I let my ego take the lead and I gave into the temptations of fulfilling a false desire. In my group of friends, I have always been the single one. I've been surrounded by my dearest and closest people, watching their beautiful love stories unfold before me. I saw them experience true love and happiness from finding their partners and all that comes with it. At the weekend gatherings, when we would all come together, have drinks and prepare to go out on a night of dancing and fun, I was the solo one. Although they never made me feel this way, I often felt like an outsider.

I related to them on a lot of different areas, of course I did. They are my tribe, the people who have always been there for me, those who know me the most and love me for who I am and I love them. But as we grow, we experience different stages of life. They were in a phase that was simply foreign to me and I was at a stage that was unfamiliar to them. Many times, I would doubt my independent fiery career driven nature, and fall for a comfortable idea of finding a partner and settling down. I thought to myself, maybe then I would be able to fit in more and share the same experience they were in. Was I supposed to be at that same stage? And so, I would pick the wrong men and get into a relationship. But of course, they never lasted, because my intention was never honest to begin with. I wasn't looking for a relationship for the right reasons but instead to simply fulfil an illusion I thought would suit my reality at the time.

I did however love one man in particular with whom I experienced many beautiful moments. He was everything many women desire: early 30's, incredibly charming, attractive, wealthy, intelligent, a smooth talker and had a great career. He was the bad boy, a confident Leo man who dated many women and broke just as many hearts. His reputation was not the best, so of course when he started courting me, I didn't think much of it. I was actually completely put off by his overly confident approach, which I found arrogant and I was not impressed with him at all. But it seemed at the time this was exactly what he was searching for, a woman who was not going to give in easily. Perhaps I was different than the rest for him and that excited him.

The courting lasted a few weeks, a time in which he would send me lovely text messages and me replying in a brief manner. I'm not sure why I engaged in conversations with him, but it seemed right and very entertaining at the time. I did agree to meet with him one day, partly because I just wanted him to leave me alone, so I had planned to tell him that I appreciated his courtship but that I was not interested in communicating further. During our first date, I got to know him on a more personal level and realized he was actually quite lovely. I was surprised about how much we had in common and he made me laugh. After a few glasses of wine, and hours of great conversation, we ended the evening with a kiss. That was it, I was now under his spell. There was something so special about him, I still cannot pin point to what it was. It seemed that the role he was playing in front of others was not necessarily congruent with who he actually was and I saw this as I got to know him more.

The moment our lips touched it felt as though the beginning to a beautiful story, one I couldn't quite figure out the plot to. I just know that our souls connected on such a deep level and it felt natural that we were to meet and be together. He made me feel beautiful inside and out, and most importantly he respected me. I would share my hopes and dreams with him and he would do the same, and it felt good to have somebody who understands me. We were both incredibly driven and curious about pushing the boundaries when it came to self-development and this I found to be rare. I felt like for the first time in my life, I was with somebody who was a soul mate. At that point, I had no clear idea of what a soul mate would be like, but if I was to describe it, for me him would be it. The relationship took off very quickly, but after only a few months, he told me that he was moving overseas for a job he was offered. As I was working in the same field and as I was hopelessly in love, I told him I would consider moving as well so we could be together and continue seeing each other. He happily agreed, and everything was set; we decided mutually we were going to take on this adventure together. As his new job required him to be there quite promptly, a month later, he boarded his flight and that was the beginning of our long-distance relationship, a time I struggled with a lot. I missed him all the time, I cried and longed for him, I would wake up and go to sleep thinking of him. I found myself constantly trying to figure out the time zones and scheduling phone calls when we were both free to speak. Looking back at that younger version of myself, I can now identify the need I had to feel loved and belong to somebody, a concept I had not realized at the time or perhaps I was afraid of admitting.

But since I planned to move as well, our relationship felt secure somehow because we had a clear outcome set in place. Only that during this time apart, I realized that if I moved, I would leave behind all of my hopes of exploring life further so that I would reach the heights I had always dreamt about since I was that little girl in Romania. I would become the girlfriend and not the woman I dreamt of being. After two months of crying and numerous Skype conversations, one day I decided this was enough and I couldn't continue. I can't explain it, it's as if a light switched on and I suddenly realized this was not the best path for me to take. So, I changed my plans of moving and instead applied for my psychology degree, one of the best decisions I had ever made for myself. I truly believe the universe pulled a very abrupt and unannounced hand break during that time because I felt almost as surprised as he was when I told him. I was so heartbroken. That beautiful love tale I imagined would happen had now become an illusion of the past. I felt like a part of me was dormant and I couldn't do anything about it. But as time went by, so did our emotions because after a while it seemed we had both moved on. Fast tracking two years forward, I was now in my third year of studies and had not spoken with him since the breakup.

Things were good and I was happy. For the first time in a long I knew I was doing exactly what I should have been in that moment. I was focused, regained my strength and I felt empowered and closer to the person who I dreamt of becoming; a strong, independent woman who could do anything she wanted. Sometimes though the universe likes to test us and just when things are going well, it pulls another hand break, just to remind us that life is not as linear as we believe it to be. This moment arrived for me when one day, out of the blue I received a message from him letting me know that he was returning to New Zealand in a few weeks. That was it, one simple text message that completely shook up everything that I had worked for in the last couple of years. I still remember contemplating if I should reply or not, but love is not rational, it's emotional and sometimes, no matter how much we want to go against the current of our emotions, it somehow pushes us towards it. It didn't take very long for us to rekindle and messaging back and forth; we decided we were going to give it another shot when he returned. It was an instant connection once again and my feelings for him blossomed quickly. He was so special for me, the first man I had loved, and I don't think we can ever forget your first true love. I was happy to know that within two of weeks I would be next to him again and we were to start a new chapter of our lives together. We made so many plans. We even decided to move in together and give it a real shot. I started looking for apartments and mentally decorating each one of them to suit our own style as a couple. At that time, I was working as a part-time counsellor in between my study days, so I had some spare time to daydream about our gorgeous new home we would share.

But his arrival was all I could think about. I had arranged to have the day off work so I could pick him up from the airport. Two days before his arrival, I had messaged him one morning to double check the time his plane was to land. Hours went by and I still had not received a reply. With my naiveté of a young woman in love, I thought maybe something happened to him or his flight. I panicked and was worried sick about him. What I didn't admit then is that deep down I knew something was wrong, not with his circumstances but with us, only to ignore my gut instinct that told me this was just an illusion and none of it was to happen. Little did I know that a reply was never to come and there I was, left like a fool. My heart felt shattered in pieces. It hurt so bad I physically felt the sensations of a true heartbreak. What was worse is the embarrassment I had to face in front of my family and friends, who when the time came asked me where he was and humiliated, I had to confess what had happened. That was a low point in my life, however one that taught me great lessons. Still I can honestly say that out of all my relationships, this is the one I feel most grateful for. Although it hurt the most, this man also gifted me with the ability to love. Until then, I had no idea what this felt like but in meeting him, my heart opened to the idea of true love and that's something to be thankful for.

Looking back now, I am happy it was him and nobody else. Although he made his fair share of mistakes, I had made mine too. I truly believe we were two people who were so right for each other but met at the wrong time. No matter how much we tried to be together, something would always get in the way. Perhaps it was our own fear, or maybe the universe stepped in.

I will never know because that experience was never mentioned again even when a few years later, out of the blue I received a Merry Christmas message from him. This time we were not going to kid one another about starting over, but instead we just kept the conversation minimal and expressed our well wishes for the festive season. The universe tested me again and this time I am proud to say I had learnt my lesson and left what once was where it should be, in the past. Deep down I think I had always hoped for us to end up together, but later on I understood that in relationships there are only so many chances two people can have at working things out and once these ran out, no matter how much you try, it will just not happen. Even at a soul level, the energy will always be there but with time it can become weaker. He was the man who I loved the most and for whom I suffered the most. But this taught me so much and it helped me grow thicker skin. I was now aware of what a relationship required for me; that it's important to give chances to people; that you must give yourself the chance to be happy. I learnt that it's ok to feel vulnerable and to suffer in a moment of weakness because it is after the dark days, the brightest light appears to bring clarity onto our path.

There is no heartbreak without love, just as there is no love without the experience of heartbreak. The beauty in relationships lies in the balance of the two. To fear heartbreak, is to be afraid of love because the more you focus on what you don't want to experience, the quicker it will come to you. Relationships are not meant to be easy, they are simply meant to be. Whatever relationship you have experienced, you were meant to do so at that point in your life. Whether it was for a season or longer, there was certainly a reason that came with it. I'm not sure if there is such a thing as everlasting love between two people, but what I am certain of is that two souls that long to meet will no doubt do so. It may not be at the time we expect it to happen or even in the hopelessly romantic way we imagine it to be, but if we focus our energy on that one special soul, the connection is already made on an energetic level. It may take weeks, months, years when this connection comes into a physical dimension. Sometimes it may not even come in this lifetime, but perhaps in the next, when the souls of course once again return to continue the journey from we left it. During this powerful soul connection, there is a higher power that decides when the two people will come together. This powerful decision is made by the universe, the space where as a collective we all share our energies which vibrate of one another. Some stick together, some bounce away from others, but rest assured the souls that are meant to rekindle or join forces for the first time, no doubt their time will come. Whilst nobody is perfect, the souls are complete and pure. This is why when two people first meet; there is an almost innocent, childlike feeling of excitement, fun and joy.

That is the moment the souls come into proximity of one another and these external outbursts of emotion are a result of this closeness. As the relationship progresses, we become so distracted with everything else that's not important and it is then when things start to fall apart. And whilst the souls will still remain connected, the physical self of a person can fall so trapped into its ego that they will reject the purity of the relationship that once was perfect. We pick up bad habits from other couples, we listen too much to what others have to say, to take their advice when we should know better because the truth is deep down within each one of us. We place importance on stupid things like status, sense of style and whose turn it is to do the washing. And the worst, we start to take for granted the qualities they possess which we once appreciated the most. Why is it that with habit, we let ourselves doomed by that little voice that screams at us that the grass is greener? Is it that we want to see a greener grass or is it that we fail to see just how good things are the way they are? When fear dominates, darkness takes over and the person we once were, can turn into a complete stranger with self-created illusions. We lose ourselves and start a game to keep ourselves entertained. Only that in this game there will be no winner, because in love and war, both people fall in suffering. It may not manifest on a physical level, but the souls feel it, and with each attempt to burn something that should light brighter, we deplete the strong, pure energy our souls are meant to blossom further.

It's almost amusing to me to think that at times we chase somebody desperately in the hopes they will notice us. We do anything to make it work, even though there is no real existing foundation between the two. You cannot make somebody love you, nor you can force yourself to do so. On a collective level, we are all a small fraction of this planet and even though we are together in this universe on a physical dimension, it doesn't mean that on a spiritual level we must connect also. Many souls may have never connected and maybe they will one day or perhaps they never will. When you feel rejected, heartbroken and worthless, this actually all stems from you taking the conscious decision to go against what you know you are worthy of, further creating a dependency upon validating this self-worth. If you really think about it, why would you want to get somebody's attention who is simply not interested in you? Is it because you are determined to prove yourself that you can win this or is it because you are afraid you are not worth more? Through my many attempts at relationships, I have learned that with each one that ended, I became wiser, stronger and more lovable and most importantly, I would get closer to the one that would be a right fit, if I had learned my lessons. Whilst I experienced emotional pain through a break up, with this also came the realization of something so powerful. I accepted that I am not perfect, that I can be vulnerable and that I am worth loving just as much as I am worthy of giving love.

I used to resist breakups and chased all the wrong men, until I began to love myself, the same way as I would want somebody to love me and me them. And when this person arrives in my life, I will know it because I will be ready to share all this love with them. In my endless days as a single woman, I have learned and continue to respect myself enough to say no and to acknowledge when somebody is not serving me for my highest good or I to them. In this case, the balance is non-existent, and the relationship is built on a false intention.

Every day we are presented with the opportunity to meet new people from all walks of life. If we are truly emerged in the present, we will see these opportunities and be open to them. Every person that comes our way has done so for a reason. There are no coincidences, only the universe working its magic. Sometimes, we meet people who help us professionally; from others, we might learn lessons that we previously failed to pay attention to; some people will teach us about the beauty of being open to kindness whilst others will show us that life is not always paved with perfect moments; and then there are the most special kinds, the people who come into our lives to remind us how to love again and how it feels to be loved. These are the soul mates, the ones who we have always been connected with on an energetic level and now in the physical realm. Some of the best friendships I have created in my life were with people who I met in the simplest of circumstances. It's as if we were supposed to be there, at the same place in the same time.

I have friends in my life with whom I have shared moments with for almost two decades and regardless how long we go without talking or the physical distance between us, when we meet, everything is still the same. Others, I have only known for a couple of years, yet I feel as though I've known them my entire life. And then there are people who I've met for a week and have felt instantly connected with. Sometimes there is no need to overanalyze the reason why we meet the people we do, but instead to just let the experiences shared together flow, to just be. When I started travelling, I gained a clearer perspective on who my true friends were. This doesn't mean all the others were not real bonds; it just means that their purpose in my life and mine in theirs had come to a completion.

Whilst being away from my dearest friends, I have learned to detach myself completely of any need to be dependent on somebody's presence. Instead I came to the conclusion that when I am in the presence of these amazing people, I will truly savour it and completely live that moment. I keep the memories of these experiences close to my heart and show gratitude to these people for being in my life. I very rarely say "I will miss you" anymore.

Our souls will always be connected with one another and there is no need to interfere this beautiful energetic connection with thoughts of pity and negativity by living in the past or longing for the future. This allows me to be open every day to all the new wonderful people the universe will bring into my path. When you liberate yourself from trapping your mind into living for what once was, you welcome in the new.

TEN

BELONGINGNESS

There is no greater force of alignment with our true self than the one of belongingness. At a physical level, we are born as individuals, but on a soul level, we are part of a greater collective consciousness. On a physical dimension, we can become so self-cantered that we don't actually realize that we are simply a part of something that is bigger than us. Take a walk on the busiest street in your city and you will see just how insignificant you can be to some, yet if you are in a room full of people who know and love you, then you can feel like you matter, that you belong to somebody, that you have a purpose to be there.

And perhaps the most enlightening experience is when you take a walk on a deserted beach or in a forest, surrounded by tall trees and nature's beauty and as you look at all these amazing creations, you might just realize that you are a tiny part of a huge, loving universe. Social interactions are at the pinnacle of reminding us that to belong is to truly experience life at its highest vibration. It is not so much about who we think we are but how best we serve those around us and vice versa that creates and brings to life the meaning of our presence and those of others'.

I've had many accomplishments so far in my life that I am really proud of but I acknowledge that there are still a lot of lessons I must take on in order to bring a deeper meaning to my happiness. There is one area of my life however for which I am grateful to have experienced because it has brought me to realize just how important it is to first give love to yourself and then spread it to others. When you are alone or have been for a long time, whether it is that you've been single, travelled to many beautiful places away from your loved ones or have been focusing on your career and minimized the time you spend with your friends, there are many things that come your way that can make you feel good. Externally you may feel accomplished.

Your ego will tell you that you are doing fine and that everything is going your way because you are achieving all that you have set yourself up for. You keep striving to be the best version of yourself by continuously being victorious at everything you do but in the process, you might find yourself missing out on the experiences that will really bring you closer to yourself. At some point, we will learn that even though we can master the art of individuality and being on your own, there is still the basic human need to belong. We need our souls to constantly be nurtured so that we feel and grow within ourselves emotionally, physically, mentally and spiritually. Belongingness brings everything together. We are social beings by nature, we live in a collective universal force of energy that binds us together, that creates momentum and that spark when we connect with others. Being alone teaches you many things. At first, it can be very strange because it's like you are meeting a person for the first time, one who is always there with you and from who you cannot disconnect. It can feel quite odd in the initial stages because you don't know where to begin. So you have to start with the beginning, to get to know yourself on a personal level. You learn about what you like and what you are good at. In that moment, you realize that you have to put in an effort just as you would when you first meet somebody. You might discover that you need to respect yourself more and create a routine, which aids to your overall wellbeing and discovery of the self.

This is the primary phase in which you decide how to nurture your physical self. This could be by creating a routine in which you start working out more often to become stronger physically and look after your body in a more caring way than before. Placing a focus on your body is more important than soul-searching in the initial phase because without a healthy physical self you cannot reach to the deeper levels of yourself. This same analogy applies to the practice of yoga. First you will begin practicing the yoga poses or asanas, which help to purify the physical body and as you get more experienced in your practice, you go deeper in the mental body and the spiritual body. You have to realize that at some point, if you fall into a rut of physical procrastination, there is nobody else who can save you but you. No number of personal trainers, dieticians, healers and magic body workers will empower you to become healthier, because the real motivation and desire comes from within. There may be people, who push you, but ultimately, it's you who is driving your life vehicle and so you are the one who decides to wake up every day and do something about it.

You have to start learning how to become yourself and being alone teaches you that. It gives you the ability to look beyond what you think you want and need because you get to know different faces of yourself. You start to develop different hobbies by discovering the things you enjoy doing, which bring happiness for you. I learned that I enjoy cooking, so I began doing it more often. I realized that I enjoy meditating and with that came a passion for tarot card reading and astrology, so I started learning more about these two fields. I began reading more books and made a conscious effort of doing so because I realized it added value to my life.

Through these findings, I brought out a whole new side of myself that has been dormant in me for a long time, but which I have felt was longing to come out for quite some time. All these different areas that I discovered about myself were not possible, until I was on my own and was in a way forced to pursue and discover. Eventually, you get to know yourself so well that you actually start enjoying your own company. This is of course an ideal state, but a healthy balance needs to be created between the time spent on your own and being part of a social environment.

There is however an imbalance that can start occurring when you can become so comfortable of being on your own, that when you are part of a group, whether that is with your family, friends, in the community, at work or in a relationship, it feels as though they are invading the space that you created. So, it's very important that you are constantly working on yourself but that you can still be part of somebody else's life as well and are willing to do so. Because without the human interaction, all the self-development you are doing for yourself will not add any value to the collective consciousness we are part of within the universe we live in. We all have talents and gifts, but ultimately, we have to learn to share these with the world. We must learn to both give and receive. We must connect with others, to learn to give love and receive love. Being vulnerable in front of others takes courage and it's such a brave act. It's ok to need, and to ask for help so that we are not isolating ourselves from the rest of the world. The hard work is in discovering yourself, but the real challenge is how you apply that in this collective consciousness, as a social being.

To make the most out of any situation in your life, you must be able to first embrace the one you are in at the present moment. There is no greater shift in your mind, than it is the one of being grateful for what you have now and then embracing it. There is a big difference between being alone and being lonely. That difference is decided upon in the way you choose to group your thoughts. If you are alone and you appreciate that this time is serving you for the best, you will no doubt make this a valuable experience for you. This is when you start seeing the benefits of being alone, by focusing more on yourself, getting closer to your roots and reconnecting with your core authentic self. At the same time, you have the choice of deciding that you are lonely. This will then suggest that you feel as though there is nobody there for you and that all you have is not good enough. What you are really doing is minimizing your self-worth by deciding that it is not good enough for you to spend time with yourself, that it does not serve you for the best. To be alive is simply to live in the now. Regardless of the circumstances you may find yourself in, whether it is that you are alone or lonely, the obvious fact is that you simply are; for it is you who decides your own reality. The silence you will encounter when you are alone will bring out more noise in you than it would if you were in a crowded room, full of chattering voices.

But to reach tranquil waters, you must first face the storm. Being alone and truly embracing this will provide you with the notion that once the storm is gone, the truth will peacefully be revealed to you, a new horizon awaits, and the path will be clear. The truth is, the storm will probably never leave, but when we find the peace through the chaos, we have the power to choose how we see this storm. Too often we seek comfort in others when we feel a sense of dependency that we think would give us the validation of all we are and what we have. We long to be loved, protected and sheltered by the words of encouragement from those around us. We do this because it feels good and our ego likes to be comforted. But the most powerful healing comes when you appreciate that the love you require and the protection you seek are all within you. We fail to recognize this and the message we send out to the universe is that we are not good enough. But how can we expect a life of great abundance when we don't even acknowledge the prosperity that lies within ourselves? The social aspect of the physical dimension of the universe is there so that we can connect with others, that we share our beautiful energy and that others do the same. Instead, too many of us confuse this for a self-created dependency upon one another. We become delusional about the notion that we cannot be who we want to be, or that we are not who we are without the others or the things we acquire. The more we do this, the further away we move from our inner wisdom and authentic self. There is no greater love we will ever experience than the one we give ourselves.

Without the awareness that you have it within you to give, there is no love. To truly experience love, you need to find it from within and use it on yourself. Then you will understand what it feels like, how it is to be given love and how it feels to receive it. Until then, all the external love we perceive to have been given is simply an artificial euphoric, self-created state. Because without finding it within, we are not able to truly recognize its essence or existence. Being alone will teach you all of this and more. If you live in the moment and you acknowledge that at this point in time, whatever has happened for you is meant to bring you closer to your original self, then no doubt it will. Have trust in yourself and the universe. Then you will truly become empowered and prompted to live with no expectations, but instead with more love.

The primary basic need of belongingness will only become reality when you reach the ability to belong to yourself. Everything we perceive to be externally is only done so due to the creation of that notion within us. This means that what we see from the outside, we have created inside ourselves also. We can become one with our soul and physical self which brings out the wholeness that we are in this lifetime. We can then give love from the soul to the physical self and vice versa, which nurtures and heals all aspects of our own persona, both spiritually and physically. Self-acceptance will be born from all these aspects and when this is done, we also discover acceptance for everything outside of ourselves; Because what we see on the outside, is prompted by its existence on the inside.

THE PHYSICAL SELF

Self-development is an everlasting state of continuous shift within one's physical, mental, emotional and spiritual self. To reach the depths of its benefits, we must learn start with the top layer, and this is our physical self. Looking at yourself from your most external part doesn't require too much imagination. Instead we must simply look in the mirror and observe. Who we are on the surface, greatly suggests what is happening internally. We must always take in consideration however that things that seem to us as they are simply exist this way because of how we view them from within. So, looking in the mirror and seeing what you see is the first and easiest step to self-discovery. The eye will see what it wants to see, but the way we feel about this is always a result of the distance or closeness we have between our authentic self and the identity we have created for ourselves. Watching your reflection in the mirror, whilst standing there naked of everything to cover it, except for the flesh of your skin, what do you see? How do you feel when you take that first glance? As you continue to look, do you notice a change in your emotions? Are you feeling vulnerable, happy, content, disgusted, proud, sexy, ashamed, entitled? The start to my self-development began when I did exactly this.

I sat in the mirror and watched myself. I stood there, facing who is standing before me and really observed who I am on a physical level. Strangely enough, my first thought was that I was feeling shy, a little bit uncomfortable to stare at myself. Going beyond this phase, I continued further in seeing my body the way it is. I noticed areas that I saw as imperfect, perhaps ones that I thought I could improve on. I looked at my skin and observed my complexity. I saw myself in a light I had never yet before experienced. But seeing without feeling is simply an illusion, so I started associating feelings with what I was observing. My shyness soon turned into curiosity and further transformed into appreciation which later on brought upon self-love. It is only through these moments of self-discovery on a very basic level that I told myself that I am beautiful, in the most modest way possible. This is something you must do for yourself before you dig in any deeper. Without accepting yourself on a physical level, it will be very hard to face your emotions and internal self. To see what has been the product of your own doing from within is to accept who you are in this moment. I must stress that this has nothing to do with your colour, size, and skin but simply of what you see and acknowledging it. To become your own true self, you need to first discover what you are right now. Have I been good enough with my body? Have I been kind with my skin? Have I given myself the rest I need in order for my body to perform at its best potential? These are some of the questions that came into my mind as I was doing this self-reflection exercise.

We create expectations about how we want others to see us, and sometimes we get confused as to why they don't see what we think see. But what is it that you see they are not seeing? Are you manifesting that out there, or is it all a concept created in your mind? There is physical beauty in everything that exists. We have been created to find and appreciate this unique beauty so that we can further do so for others. By looking at our surface, over time we will see our physical self-changing and understand that our spiritual self will always remain the same as it was when it all began. Although as the physical self begins to mature, the spiritual self continues to stay pure and full of love, something that nobody could ever take away from you.

5 powerful affirmations for a healthier, happier physical self:

1. I love and appreciate my body and I give it the right foods and exercise to that it can perform better.

2. I deserve to live a healthy, happy, active lifestyle.

3. I exercise because I love and appreciate my body and overall wellness.

4. I live a healthy life because it's important to me.

5. I feel energized and productive every day because I live an active, healthy lifestyle.

CHAPTER ELEVEN

THE WAKE-UP CALL

My whole life I dreamt that one day I would have an incredibly successful career. Perhaps I associated this with power which for many years I thought would lead to happiness and confused its meaning for something that we must create for ourselves, instead of identifying that it's already within of us. At some point in our life, we will identify power with external gains like money, physical strength, wealth of things and career status but the most intense kind of power comes from within and that can only be achieved when you constantly evolve, challenge your mind to new findings, to discover things you never knew and to acknowledge that there is so much more to life than just what you already know. This can only be revealed to us when we become more in tune with the spiritual side of ourselves, which in a way is one of life's greatest achievements.

What I was sure of is that to reach even greater heights, it required a lot of sacrificing and discipline. Sacrifice can be quite a heavy word, but it is through this that we gain clarity on all we want vs all we actually need. I knew that hard work gets one far, and although I thought I have given it my all until now, when I landed this new role in Australia I was about to be reminded of how much more I had to give. I was exposed to hard work my whole life and I think it helped me to manage what was to come next. I was completely ready to start this new phase of my life, with a stronger, more experienced professional self but also beginning to getting a glimpse into my spiritual self. I began working inexplicably long days because I thought that giving my life to it would mean that I would get just as much out of it. My ego was so in control at this stage and without me realizing I was totally letting it lead the way.

There was some sort of satisfaction however I felt with this almost workaholic type of behaviour and I must admit I enjoyed it. I was exhausted but for some reason, I felt more alive than ever. I was giving it 120% every single day and I was amazed at how much more I still had to give. With every struggle, I would find myself scratching the surface even deeper, pushing my boundaries and diminishing my self-created limitations of how much I was able to take on. It hurt at times, but it felt so good because every time this happened, I was reminded just how strong I was and how much closer I was getting to who I wanted to become at that time. And it is through these times that we are required to search for that equilibrium of pain and pleasure, of satisfaction and discontent. For me, it was as if I wanted to see just how far I can push myself, because every time I had done so, there would be no breaking point, but instead a desire to go even more. But I have always respected my body and I was also able to recognize when my mind needed a break. So after long days at the office, or a stressful launch week, I would always book myself a massage, or a floatation tank session. This type of relaxation therapy was introduced to me by one of my later mentors, who always reminded me that recharging your batteries is necessary in order to continue in the race. I found myself waking up thinking about work and I would go to sleep with the same thoughts.

On Friday afternoons, when the team would invite me to the local pub for an end of the week drink, I would kindly decline, to ensure everything was in place and all work has been prepared for the weekend. And when I would get home from the office, I'd treat myself to an iced skinny latte from the café down the road from my apartment and then I would continue to reply to emails and catch up on more work. Many people might see this as an obsession, but I learned that to become amazing at something, a certain level of obsession was necessary. I once read somewhere a quote that really stuck out to me and it is the only way I could best describe the state I was in "Some might call it an obsession, but I call it determination". Maybe this doesn't make sense for everyone, but to me it made perfect sense.

I think sometimes people are afraid to push through once they reach a certain level of commitment and achievement. But this in itself means that you have to stay focused no matter what the challenges, and for some reason I never had trouble doing do. Don't get me wrong, at times I doubted this, especially when I had to cancel on catch ups with friends or dinner plans with my boyfriend at the time. One of my ex boyfriends with whom I had my first relationship with in Melbourne broke up with me because he said I was giving more attention to my work than to our relationship. I was confused by his decision and his reason, because in my view I was balancing out both as well as I could. Now that I look back at this relationship, I could see the disconnect that occurred between us. I was content with my work life and was happy to be with somebody who I thought appreciated me for who I was. Later on, he confessed that the real reason he ended our relationship was because he felt incredibly intimidated by my internal strength and infinite ambition I possessed and as he put it, he just simply couldn't keep up with it. My drive and determination brought out some sort of insecurities within him that he could simply not get past.

I actually appreciated his honesty but was not happy about the break up. In fact, I suffered a lot, but my love for what I did kept me going because I knew that this is a big part of me and I needed to explore it more. My mind was focused on something else and I made it my mission to give it my all no matter what. Compromise is an important part of relationships, and although I was ready to compromise on some aspects, my career was not one of them. I wanted to push beyond my limits and the more I did, the less I was afraid of doing so. But trust me when I say this, it was not easy. I felt alone at times and completely isolated by all that was considered the norm.

I was offered the role of global marketing manager for an international leading brand in its category; I was beyond excited about my new title but most of all I was grateful to be part of an entrepreneurial company yet again with two amazingly talented co-founders, who both inspired me in their own ways. The responsibilities I knew previously, multiplied overnight. I was now responsible not only for a marketing department and the team, but also for other areas of the business and I was the accountable one for all the brands' campaigns worldwide. I cannot even explain to you how everything changed. I was now constantly working, with very little time for myself. For some this may sound somewhat sad, but I was pleased with my achievements; it was ultimately what I wanted. Being a highly driven individual, I decided to focus all my time on work.

I knew for some reason that this part of my life was meant to be dedicated mostly to it and I listened to my gut as I always do. I had my work laptop on me at all times, which meant that I could work from anywhere, anytime and this suited me just fine. The two co-founders were incredibly clever in business and very passionate about what they were doing, and this transferred onto me. When I departed from my last job, I was left with an uncontrollable fear of doubting that I would never find such a great company to be part of again and most importantly Rob my last mentor, was hard to replace. I was afraid I wouldn't find another person to learn from, someone who believes in me as much as my first mentor did. But once again, the universe showed me its kindness and put me in a fast paced, global company, with the job title I wanted, a decent salary and with two leaders who inspired me greatly and who pushed me every day to get outside of my comfort zone and reach for greatness.

Mark and I didn't see eye to eye in my first couple of months with the company. A very assertive and straight up man, Mark knew what he wanted and a blonde newbie in Australia wasn't going to impress him from the beginning. A tall middle-aged man, with a strong, loud voice and a very direct approach was quite different from what I was used to until now. But I appreciated his honesty and somehow, I found it quite refreshing. Although slightly confused about what I was getting myself into, all I knew is that I wasn't going to let this affect me; after all I had come so far and worked too hard to let somebody's perception of me weigh me down. I had never met somebody like him before and I don't know if I ever will do, but I knew he was an extremely successful businessman and also spiritual and that was enough for me to know that I wanted to work for him.

I was interested in learning and bettering myself in the business field, and sometimes that doesn't come in the most tranquil waters; but I had learned that his approach would actually suit me just fine. I wasn't looking for somebody to pat me on the back every time I did something good, but instead a mentor who would challenge my limitations so that I could learn to go even further. In my first interview with him, all he wanted to know was my life path number as he is passionate about numerology and it's his way of telling if somebody would be good enough for the job, I suppose one could call it a more spiritual type of psychometric testing, at least that's how I viewed it. I still remember the shock on his face when I began telling him all about my number. I too am passionate about numerology and at least for the beginning we had something in common. I was taught to be humble, caring and compassionate in my leadership approach and Mark was the complete opposite.

He was loud, brutally honest and somewhat cold in his delivery. But we both shared something, and that was our good intention, passion for what we did and drive to get results. To this day he tells people that he was never wrong about anybody who walked into his office, except for one and that's me. He didn't see my potential in the beginning but as time went by, he was proven wrong. I have to admit I was grateful for his approach because it really taught me to believe in myself even more and to always produce high quality work because the results will always follow regardless of how much or how little others think of me. As time went by, we began working closely together and it is then I got to know him better.

Mark was the kind of boss who never accepted excuses, and this opened my eyes to see just how much we really can do if we eliminate our negative beliefs about what we think is impossible. If I thought I couldn't do something, he would challenge me to find a way, and surprisingly most of the time I did. I guess he realized my potential because he sort of took me under his wing and began giving me more responsibilities for other parts of the business. To me, he was a great teacher, the kind who would explain the process once and then let me give it a try and just do it and if I made a mistake, he would always be happy about it because to him mistakes are opportunities to learn. Patience was not his strongest trait and his speech was firm and straight to the point, almost like the sports coaches who scream and shout at the athletes but do so only to get the best results out of them, the ones who help create superstars in the making.

His trust in my abilities gave me a confidence boost to expand myself even further and see how much I can accomplish. He taught me that the impossible is possible and that I should never give up on something I believe in because there will always be a way. He taught me confidence in my business approach and encouraged innovation from me. He challenged me to think outside of the box and to not be afraid to look like a fool, because only then I could learn. As "scary" as some people may see him due to his highly direct and unfiltered approach, I saw through all that noise and realized behind that there is a soul that just wants to empower and help others and he genuinely did, but he did it in his own way which is why most people don't get it.

I learnt to focus on what he was saying and not necessarily how he was delivering it and for me this worked. I don't think there are many people who dare to work with him directly, but those who do are the ones who are on their way to greatness. Because to be able to understand such an approach, you must have high levels of self-awareness and responsibility and you must be able to put your ego aside and live from your truth, because he will challenge it. I had both and working for him reminded me of that. He opened my eyes to everything I knew was possible but did not dare to get close to. I learned from him that if you want to make something happen, you just have to make a plan and go for it regardless of the setbacks because these are part of the process.

And then there was Sam, the creative genius as I called him. Sam was the other co-founder and the man who believed in me from the beginning. Although Mark didn't see much in me at first, Sam was the one who convinced him that I would be good enough for the role and I will be forever grateful to him for doing so. Very friendly and approachable, Sam and I got on well from the beginning. He was interested in sports as I was, so we would often have long conversations about motivation and sportsmanship. Sam was kind and his ability to create concepts out of nothing really intrigued me. He really was a creative genius and I was always amazed at the beauty he crafted with his designs. His commercial eye was so sharp.

A life path number 7 like myself, which is the seeker of truth and the philosopher, Sam and I would sometimes sit for hours at the office and discuss life, the mind and concepts of motivation and success which would inspire us to create marketing campaigns and the business strategy. He taught me so much about the importance of staying true to who you are and looking within. He taught me to open my creativity and to never be afraid of trying. I learned how to be more commercially savvy by working with him and to be flexible in my approach when it comes to business. I also learnt from him not to take everything so seriously and to have fun with work because creativity will then blossom even more.

Both humble and chaotic in their own ways, I couldn't understand how these two got along so well as they were complete opposites. But I learned that in business you need that difference and the tension it brings is what cements a strong foundation. I realized then that the universe listened to what I had hoped for, and instead of giving me one mentor, it unselfishly provided me with two. At 28 years old, I was leading the marketing strategy for a successful global company and it felt good. I got myself a small, brand new apartment in one of the best neighbourhoods in Melbourne and sometimes I had to stop and really take it all in. I truly feel grateful for all experiences I have encountered for they have helped me discover myself in so many ways of which I never knew before.

For most of the time, I was always the first in the office and almost always the last one to leave (a great habit I picked up from Rob). And if I left earlier, I would continue to work remotely. I answered all of my bosses' phone calls, regardless if they were on the weekends or very early in the morning. I was working seven days a week because since day one I did not have even one day without checking and replying to emails. I was doing so many things at once and am still amazed to this day of how I did so much in such little time. But I was driven and determined, and this is what I had hoped for. It was all I dreamed about for such a long time, so why wasn't I feeling as happy as I thought I would be?

There comes a time in our life when we have to really assess what exactly we want to be doing but most importantly find the reason and intention behind it. This realization can take us by surprise and create some confusion amongst all the certainty we thought we have established for ourselves. Everybody reaches their tower moment, and this can happen many times, because without the universe shaking up the foundations we build, we cannot grow nor we can truly find our original self.

When you become good at what you do, it's almost effortless to fall into the trap of believing that is what you are meant to be doing. You can fall captive in a world of comfort you may not even identify as it is. You become better and better at it and the more you do it the more you will want to excel in that field because the ego is the driving force and the superficial satisfaction that comes with things well done tricks us into believing it is what we are meant to be doing. When however, we feel a shift and we begin to question ourselves, the light comes so brightly that it can blind us for a moment. When you reach this moment, as I have, the most important question to ask yourself would be "What is it that's deep down, within you wanting to come out and burst with all that love and good intention to create something that is meant to be for you?

"How is it that you will best serve for what is around you and bring value to your significant existence in the universe?" As our soul communicates with our physical self through our body, more specifically our intuition, we will receive the guidance when we are ready to be open to it. I confused my success of being a great marketing manager for what I was meant to be doing with my life.

I thought because I became so good at it, this meant that it was my purpose. It had to be right? But it didn't feel right to me. Although I had two great mentors, a talented team, a beautiful office, a decent salary and the freedom to be in and out of the office, something from within was pulling me away from it. I had everything I thought I wanted, but was it really what I truly wanted, from my most authentic self? I had lost all implementation of my creativity and was now responsible for ensuring the team I was managing was putting theirs in practice. I became an execution machine, ticking off deadlines and negotiating collaborations in almost a robotic kind of way. I had so many things on my to do list that I felt like I couldn't do anything else, but those and that made me feel trapped. I had so much creativity to offer, but I couldn't find the time to make it happen because of continuously pending activities that had to be ticked off. And of course, when you work for somebody else, you must always go by what they want. I felt stressed and this showed through the breakouts on my skin which had never happened before. At times, I felt physically ill at the thought of going into the office in the morning because I was so overwhelmed about this change that was taking place inside of me. I loved what

I was doing but I was exhausted, and it no longer felt right for me. It's as if I was trying to hold onto something but at the same time a greater force was pulling me in a different direction. I believe that up until this point, I was absolutely meant to go through this experience, however I felt as though something else was now to follow.

It all didn't make sense to me because although I was shining and doing well, inside I was feeling betrayed. I had lied to myself and in the end, I became the fool, but this in itself was a blessing. Another one of my favourites, the fool card is the first in the tarot-spread decks. It is numbered 0 because everything begins from the fool, and the card to follow is the wonderful Magician, the energy of manifestation and creating magic with all the resources and universe being on your side. The fool might not have a clue about where it's going, but one thing he is aware of is that the universe is on his side and the doors to whatever he's about to embark on will open. The fool significance is the start of a new journey and diving into the unknown, one which you not only dip your toes into, but innocently jump into it, regardless of what's to come because the fool trusts himself and all that is around him. The universe has a great way of knocking on your door as soon as you start taking off the course or feel as though you are doing so. It might give you a taste for it only at first, but you will soon find yourself parting ways with what is no longer serving you. The signs will start appearing and the soul's guidance will become more powerful and no matter how much you will try and ignore these, at some point you will get your clarity. You will feel confused and sometimes even scared, but you must always look within, find your truth and acknowledge it. It's there and has always been. This job helped me find mine and I realized that this was not the path I should continue walking on because my soul was not being listened to.

My whole life up until this point I had created an idea of what my life should be based on my desires of being successful, and it is only when I got everything I thought I wanted, the realization came to me that this persona I created and the lifestyle I had built was not congruent with my core self, but instead a product of my ego's selfish needs. I identified this because I realized no matter how much I was accomplishing, it didn't feel enough for me anymore and I became tired of this cycle. I had pushed myself through all the challenges and achieved the career status I had dreamt about for that stage in my life and enough financial wealth to do what I wanted, but I wasn't happy. I was spending 80% of my day in the office or working and it felt like I was in a box, missing out of the beautiful nature and things waiting for me outside of these four walls. Every day I would enthusiastically jump out of bed for my early morning workout and meditation session and I would feel inspired to explore the world and myself, to live authentically but an hour later I would go to the office, turn on the lights, sit at my desk and live most of my day like this, and so all my inspiration would be gone. Has this really become my life? I simply couldn't relate to this lifestyle anymore. I realized my life was completely out of balance because I had ignored the beautiful aspects of it by working myself to the bone. And I was doing it for somebody else; I was devoting most of my previous time working towards somebody else's dreams and this left little time for my own. I started thinking to myself, if I would accord even half of this commitment to my own dreams instead of theirs, how would my life be then? And that's when it hit me, my wake-up call had knocked so loudly that it now tore down every single wall I had put up to ignore it.

I had successfully completed one cycle of my life and was now faced with the opportunity to start again, this time guided by my true self and not my ego's needs to satisfy and make me feel more important by reaching a higher social status. I was not just an execution machine; my creativity was dying to manifest itself externally and this force pushed me to start writing again. It opened my eyes to the person I have always been but was not able or brave enough until now to live as that. Once I had discovered this, I found a new sense of excitement and I was eager to explore my true self without any expectations but to simply let it shine. I knew it was exactly what I was meant to be doing; it felt as though I had been aiming to reach this moment my entire life. As I look back over the years, I realized this was what I had always done however manifested it in different fields; that the practice of writing was apparent in all I was doing and now I had finally come to understand this. It's not my sole purpose, but it is a part of me that is authentic and original to my soul. Through this realization, I was able to identify that I was already complete and that I just needed to start focusing on me, the things I loved doing and be the person I truly am, without needing to become somebody else, or becoming a more glamorous version of myself. There was no need to prove to myself or to others anything; it was simply the idea of living as myself with the soul as my torch to light up the path I am walking on.

There are so many areas of life I wanted to explore but kept putting them off until that "one day" and I was done with this ignorance and decided that the "one day" is now. This internal change brought to an end my time at the company and a new-found courage to start exploring life in a more authentic way as the person I am with the wisdom gained from all my experiences so far. I took the decision to part ways and to follow my heart and passions, not to achieve a specific status but to simply let myself enjoy the experiences as they will manifest. Somehow, I was completely sure that this was going to be one of the best decisions I would ever make for myself in my life.

TWELVE

EMOTIONAL BEHAVIOURS

PASSION

The most successful people I have met didn't come from wealthy backgrounds, but they were rich in passion and joy for life. The abundance that stems from passion is one that comes with a continuous flow of positive energy that helps create opportunities and discover solutions to what one considers as challenges. Everything that comes from the heart is genuine and pure. When we align ourselves with our heart's desire, we transmit waves of good intention.

This is one of the ingredients towards not only happiness, but for connecting with our soul. Passion keeps our dreams alive and our vision steady. When you are passionate about something, regardless what may be in the way, you know it's possible to get it. And if it feels impossible, you will break the barriers to make it happen because that's what true authenticity flourishes. Through passion, we can find peace that allows us to appreciate all that we have in the present moment. With it comes a sense of ease towards all that comes our way. One can often confuse passion with a greedy desire of wanting something for the sakes of feeling complete. But as human beings, we are already complete and our journey is not so much about finding people or experiences to make us feel this way, but instead to find and recognize our true purpose, what we came here to learn and what we are needed to teach.

My dream of being on a plane often and flying to beautiful places came to fruition when I was accepted for a flight attendant role. I was 20 years old and had no care in the world. I had so much energy and joy for this role and as soon as I began doing it, I knew it was the right thing for me at that time. As I was working at different hours than majority of my friends, I spent most of my time on planes and here I made new friends who were sharing the same passion as I was at the time. Being stuck in a metal tube at 30,000 feet is not necessarily everyone's definition of peace, but whenever I was up in the air I felt at my most tranquil. There's something very calming about floating in the clouds, being surrounded by people and doing something you know you enjoy. I met people from all walks of life.

Some of them were enthusiastic about their holidays to come, whilst others were travelling for business and simply wanted to be left alone. But up there, in the sky, I learned to get to know people, to speak with everybody and most importantly to listen. As a career, flight attending can be underestimated by some people, but having done it, I can say there is nothing glamorous or easy about it. The training can take up to six weeks or more and it comes with a demanding schedule. Flight attendants have the responsibility of serving passengers, but they are also there to comfort those who feel afraid of flying and most importantly they are there to ensure that the passenger's safety comes first. I loved this feeling of being able to serve to people.

It was one of the most enlightening moments of my life. Sometimes, my mind drifts back to my 20-year-old self, dressed in a beautiful uniform with the perfect make-up and hair do, walking up and down the aisle, smiling at everyone. I loved everything about it. Although it was a passion of mine, it doesn't necessarily mean that I had to carry on doing this for the rest of my life. We can find passion in many areas of life, each one providing us with joy and lessons from which we can open our eyes to new experiences. We can get a glimpse of introduction for a part of our self we never knew was there and from this will stem passion for other avenues, which we can explore later on. Passion brings out the love we have inside and this creates a positive spark within the universe therefore within us.

REGRET

In moments of doubt, I always find myself reaching out for answers in nature, the only truth we all share collectively. We all see the world differently based on our unique perceptions that stem from self-created internal systems. These are customized systems that hold our beliefs and values based on experiences that influence and lead to our behaviors. Our realities differ because our experiences are unique and different. We see, think and feel about everything that surrounds us in the way that fits within our own way of perceiving the world. But one of the only realities we agree on and share in the same way is nature.

We see everything as it is. We see the sun as the sun and feel the rain as the rain. Nature is pure and filled with beautiful energy from the earth's essence, which gives us grounding. It's no wonder then that when we spend enough time outdoors, surrounded by mother earth's finest creations and embracing the fresh air, something powerful happens. A swift motion of positive energy from nature meets our soul's energetic field and creates a frequency in which they become intertwined. As nature's energy is pure, it holds more strength than ours, and so we are able to release blockages within our energetic field that may have occurred over time; and then clear these with the powerful new energy unselfishly given to us by nature.

We are provided with a reinvigorating burst of fresh feeling that only ads more grounding and stability to our current state. It makes us feel good and connects our spiritual self, with the emotional, mental and physical parts of the self. It is in these moments that we can become most inspired because through this we come closer to connecting with our original self. If we only had the courage to let go of expectations and material desires and simply just be in nature, it is the closest we will ever come in contact with the purest form of energy on this physical dimension.

Moments of uncertainty are inevitable. As human beings, we are faced with different situations every moment of our existence. We must make decisions, which sometimes can appear to be unbearable. We can take these so suddenly, that the realization of what has come out of it only concludes itself as the aftermath occurs. Regret will only burden on you. To hold onto regret is like carrying heavy baggage on your back. The more you add to it, the heavier it gets and the harder it is for you to move forward. If we see time as an illusion, then what has happened has already come and gone, it is no longer part of the present.

So why then do we feel the need to give ourselves unnecessary importance and live with selfishness by obsessing over decisions that have already passed? We do this without realizing just how much we take what we have for granted and that life keeps on moving, with or without us keeping up with its pace. When thoughts of regret keep recurring within your present, you are no longer living in the now. You are choosing to live an experience, which is already non-existent and so the illusion of it takes over. All of this for one simple reason, the fact that we are not honest enough to face ourselves, accept what has been, acknowledge what has come and continue for what is. We choose our own reality. We are responsible for the events in our life because they are the consequences of our own actions. These consequences are congruent with the lessons we have come to learn in order for our soul's journey to continue on its quest for finding its true meaning within the physical dimension and in its current physical body. We have what we have because of the intentions we have put out in the universe and the energy we chose to release, but also because of what we are meant to experience but cannot see for ourselves. We see what we choose to create; it's just that simple!

This however doesn't make us robots. We are emotional beings, just as we are spiritual and cognitive. Our states influence the decisions we take greatly, and no matter how much we strive to take the ones we believe are correct, at times we won't because they are merely part of our perception. This of course can happen by getting distracted from all that is insignificant and could impede our progression towards the truth. It's all part of that bigger picture we are walking towards. Sometimes we will only find out by taking the detours. The soul comes back together with our physical self to teach us many lessons, but most importantly so that we can bring the value we are here to manifest, in this lifetime and this body. This can only occur by taking on the adventure, no matter how bumpy it may be. The soul has come to complete its mission and regardless of any conditions, it will hold onto that and eventually, we will find it. It is our role, through our physical self, to use our best resources given and make this happen.

I've made many mistakes in my life so far and I'm sure I will continue to do so. Perhaps my biggest mistake has been not to trust in myself enough. I used to internalize everything. I never enjoyed showing vulnerability because this to me represented weakness. I rarely exposed my true emotions to others. I conditioned myself to put on a brave face no matter what the situation. When I felt pain, I would turn this externally into a feeling of ease not because I didn't want to deal with my problems, nor because I was ashamed; but because I didn't want to burden others. Growing up in an Eastern European environment, somehow, I became tougher than perhaps I should have. Although I perceived this as being toughness, internally I was emotional and sensitive, a blessing I could not recognize for a long time. I most certainly had to learn how to deal with uncomfortable situations on my own.

But through all of this, I came to value myself. I learned that I can rely on my own and that I am strong enough to look after myself. I also experienced being vulnerable and learnt to nurture myself and appreciate my sensitivity. I began loving myself and realized that being vulnerable didn't mean being weak, but instead open and braver than ever. Only those who can show their true emotions can live from an authentic space. If you can face yourself for what you are, through practicing self-love and care, by experiencing the fear when you discover your internal wounds and learn how to heal, this means you are a warrior. And the most beautiful aspect that comes out of it of it is that once you have experienced this, you can pay it forward by helping others nurture, heal and find themselves. I learned that it's ok to ask for help because that meant connecting with others. Aren't we all here to inspire one another? After all, this is the magic of human connection. It is the differences amongst ourselves that bring to surface our unique ability to simply spark a glimpse of hope to see and reach each other's potential; to give and to receive love; because at the core of every human being, there lies kindness and love.

CONFLICT

I've never really liked the idea of conflict, I'm not sure anybody does. Although manifested in many different ways, conflict creates the same outcome for everybody. There is no such thing as winning a fight because the internal damage caused by arguing causes a strong negative impact for the individuals involved and the environment they are in. This depletes the energy of love and pureness from within and instead it continues to get repressed. Polluted with the negative energy that comes from it all, a bubble of tension is created that further causes a blockage inside of our body on an energetic level. As the energy is held into this place of constraint, the soul's ability to communicate with us via our intuition becomes weaker and a disconnect from the self is created. The ego will then rise to the occasion by taking charge of our behaviour and just like the sport coaches who sit on the side line of a game and shout and the players, the ego will make noise loud enough for the individual to react.

If we look at the animal kingdom, the lion is known as the king of the jungle. Although most animals fear the lion for its strength and careless ability to do whatever it takes to get what it wants, the lion has one scope only. It is driven by the intention to protect and survive. The lion will fearlessly go hunting to catch whatever it can in order to feed its cubs and keep their clan alive. The lion is also brave enough to step outside of its comfort zone and make it known that its territory should not be invaded upon from other animals around it. Just like the lion, our ego serves to protect and keep us alive. It does so by bringing out a defensive, side of ourselves in order to mask away our vulnerability to face and accept the truth.

Conflict happens when people are denying themselves from the truth and ignore to accept it as it is. People who argue fail to see that there will be no victory from the battle's outcome, but simply a boost of pride and rise in the ego, none of which serve us for the greater good. What we see as the truth is solely based on our perception, it is the way each mind individually pertains and reacts to any external stimulus presented. On a lower vibration, conflict can bring to light the things we may have been too afraid to speak up about and sometimes the ego, in small doses can help us address these. But when conflict creates pain and hurt to others, it goes against the principle of why we are here.

The idea of conflict makes me feel uncomfortable, not because I am afraid to see or speak the truth, but because of what it actually creates. I never liked conflict. I view it as a battle of egos which turns out to be completely unnecessary. I have had my fair share of arguments with close and dear people in my life, and have lost friends because of pointless debates. This usually occurred in the heat of the moment, when faced with challenging views, defensively we would say things to one another that created a separation. And whilst words can be forgotten, the experience caused by them will always remain part of us. Over the years, as I have been getting to know myself better and became more spiritually aware, I realized that conflict is an act of disrespecting the other person's point of view and also our own. Who am I to judge, or deny somebody from their own truth? And if I can rely on my truth as my own, not needing validation from others, then it must be known within me and that's the main experience it will bring.

When we stop judging and learn that everybody has a unique view of the world, we stop the conflict and instead learn to listen. We start sharing our ideas with others and it becomes quite a nice experience of human bonding and connection, regardless if there is mutual agreement or not. When we practice listening, we open our hearts to those around us who wish to be heard, not to change our opinion about something, but simply because they want to share their own truth. We don't have to like it, agree with it or accept it, but we can listen to it and just move on. Anger is the result of so much suppressed energy, of insecurity and fear from within a person. What causes the anger a person is experiencing is not something external, but instead their own reaction to what has happened outside of their body and mind. This reaction can be due to the disconnect one has with their own self, which creates confusion and fear. If we are happy with our truth and know that it does not cause any harm to others, why do we need to impose it upon others? Everybody has the right to think and feel as they wish, for nobody knows where they've been and where their journey is to lead. Acting from a place of anger, despair, regret and other negative self-created frames of mind or emotional states, can cause terrible harm to the self and those around.

These are just lavish ways of behaviour which take us further away from our own truth and instead step into a zone of self-centeredness that can ultimately be of detriment. As a collective, we are members of the universe, a space much broader than what we believe it to be. The world that we see exists through our eyes, but some people fear of looking beyond this dimension, because this requires them to open not only their vision but also their heart. We are here to be of service to each other and to the environment and the only way we can do this successfully is by respecting ourselves enough to understand that there is more than each one of us can perceive. We live through our senses and believe this allows us to live a full life of contentment and hope, but we should also be open to the possibility that there is more than what we think there is. The life philosophies each one of us live by are created by the many different experiences we have come on this planet to have. Therefore, it is ironic that we create judgement against one another, without having experienced what the other has. I wonder what the world would be like if we were only brave enough to just listen to others' sharing their experiences without the need to question it.

We can only understand this concept if we have the courage to look beyond the meaning of our own experiences and understand that there was a lesson to learn from it in order to move onto the next set of experiences to come.

THIRTEEN

THE REBUILDING PHASE

Perhaps the most beautiful aspect of life is that we can reinvent ourselves at any point we decide to do so. With every breath we take, we activate the life unselfishly given to us and continue to exist both energetically and physically in this limitless, beautiful universe. We have the ability to reconstruct our life based on who we are and how far along the journey of discovery we have come. With every challenge and opportunity, we continue to dig in deeper and discover more information of the self which brings us closer to realizing our authenticity and the purpose we have come to be of service with.

The most astonishing thing I have discovered so far in my life, one that is of great simplicity, that although we all have a purpose, we can discover this by being courageous enough to not deny ourselves from the experiences we are given and to see that it can be manifested through many different aspects. The soul's mission is set, and we can take various ways that will lead us to opportunities which will give us the ability to bring it to light. The truth is we all play a significant role in the universe for if we didn't, we wouldn't exist, just as everything else that has created to be part of it does.

Through every experience we take part in, we grow spiritually, sometimes unconsciously and without having full awareness that this happens. Self-development is often regarded to be quite a difficult process simply because we are not used to understand nor explain life and our existence on this planet this way. We fear to see reasoning because we would then have to face ourselves. Spirituality awakens when we understand our truth and meaning on this planet. People can find this in different ways and through different practices, and they may call it otherwise, but the connection one gains with the self and all that surrounds them as well as the reasoning for it all, that is what spirituality brings to us.

We have the power within ourselves to both create and destruct. We can only do so by simply deciding what it is that we want to do and how we choose to react to all that is presented to us in the form of life experiences. We have the choice of deciding who we want to be and how we want to live just as we have the choice to live in ignorance and fear. In the first instance, we can begin doing so energetically, by listening to the feeling that comes from within. We can then manifest it as a visualized image we create based on this feeling and finally we can involve our cognitive self to believe this is who we are. The human brain has the ability to dissect and generalize information based on what it believes we are meant to focus on and this further influences how we view the information. When there is guidance from within that brings to our awareness the need to act upon something we feel so deeply connected with, on a physical dimension we can start living it. We can choose to live in light and see our reality as it is, recognizing the magic of creation and the limitless possibilities that we hold. Or we can choose to live in darkness, to reject the beauty that lies before our eyes, by being blinded from an egotistical view of desire and temptation. Everything is simply as it is and our way of interpreting it is what bring meaning to it all. We hold the key to every door we wish to unlock, but are rarely brave enough to actually go ahead and open it. A vision has no depth nor much meaning without the action of bringing it to life. Everybody can imagine and see, just as they have the power to create, but fail to distinguish the two and the actual meaning behind each one.

One morning, I woke up and I said to myself that I am a writer. I can't exactly recall if I had dreamt something about this the night before or if there were other factors that woke me up to this realization. I have lived my whole life striving to become a version of myself that I had seen as successful, one that was to excel in many areas of life and conquer my throne as the main character of my play, which I call my life. Throughout the different adventures I had embarked on, and the various struggles encountered, I had always found myself with an uncontrollable need to write. And although the practice itself was apparent in all aspect I had gone through, I never quite took the responsibility upon it and accepted the fact that it is my own self who can start living as this persona of a writer. I knew it was my calling, but I had not acted on it in a way one should when they find their truth. From a young age, I had tried to make it into a career, without actually acknowledging that it is my lifestyle that I need to live it as and not necessarily as a profession as such. I looked for a reward, to become a writer for magazines, or maybe newspapers who would pay me to write but I never quite made those specific spectrums because my message was not congruent with the one I was supposed to achieve. I started my own blog when I was 18 years old and continued to write hundreds of blogs, in a time when blogging wasn't considered to be something of too much influence, it certainly wasn't a trendy thing to do and back then there were no Insta influencers. I wrote about everything, relationships, breakups, studying, struggles and all other life encounters that I had the knowledge of back then.

But as the popularity of my blog was growing, my inspiration of keeping my message authentic to my heart took a back seat, and instead I began writing about things I thought people would be more interested in, lighter than my usually creative and deep style of writing. And it was then I noticed a significant drop of interest from my readers. I had gone against my true creativity, and the results showed. After four years, I decided to close that blog. What I was writing about was so far away from what my true self was longing to share in the hopes to bring light and inspiration for others from lessons of my life I had gained clarity from. This confusion caused me to stop and rethink my passion for the craft. I was a young, inexperienced woman who just wanted to write, but had no idea where to start. But as I began working in public relations, my writing came back and again I found myself writing for magazines and publications for entertainment purposes, about things that I had no deep interest or curiosity about. Once again, I felt defeated and betrayed my own truth. But it is these experiences that have taught me what the message of my craft is supposed to be and why it is important for me to continue to write and without these experiences I probably wouldn't have realized this. And finally, as I began my journey of self-discovery I realized that I had not stayed true to what my essence was about. I was afraid to even think of myself as a writer because I felt a disconnection with my work.

But for some reason, years later on that morning when I woke up and I decided that I would no longer deprive myself from my own truth, so I turned on my laptop and began writing. This time, I wrote about something that had meaning and felt natural to me. It was like a wave of inspiration that had been dormant for a lifetime and it was now all coming out. There were days when I would write for hours and hours, with just a brief break to have a snack and recharge. I felt as if my purpose was shining in front of me and this time I wasn't looking for any reward, but instead I was just driven by doing something that I was meant to be doing. A year later, I found myself writing the end of the book and submitting it to the publisher. What happened is that I had finally understood that this was me all along, but I was not yet ready to believe this information and accept it. Perhaps I was scared that my writing was not good enough or that my works were not going to be published; but what I had discovered that morning was that I denied myself from it all for far too long and that I let the self-created scenarios of failure get to me. I thought because I had no book published yet that I wasn't considered or equipped enough to call myself a real writer. But then I shifted my mentality and decided to start writing my book not so that I could get a reward at the end by being published, but instead because I just wanted to write. I no longer focused on the outcome although I was very much aware of it, but I had decided to put my focus on the action.

The more I did this, the less I doubted my abilities because it was now part of my routine and I quickly became disciplined with it. The information is always with us and the great thing is that we have access to it whenever we want it. My whole life writing was always part of me, I just never really lived as it was. But when I consciously decided that I was already what I had aspired to become, the inspiration came to me and so did the opportunities.

There are moments in life when we get a very brief glimpse into the truth. We might not recognize it but if we stop the chatter and all the external glamour for just one second, we may just understand it. Everything that we aspire to be is already part of us so long we are not led by the ego. Regardless how it may all turn out, the more we follow that gut feel, the closer we get to what we are meant to see. When we stop and just wait in silence for the advice to come from within, it's there, it always has been. We know what the next course of action is so why are we so afraid to follow it? External manifestations of our successes present themselves as material things we have gained from our victory, but are they really what we are meant to gain? This then complicates the simplicity of purpose, because when we search for a reward, we lose the essence of its meaning and limit its value. Life is an exploration of the self, an adventure we share with others on a never-ending road that we might think will lead to nowhere, but it is not about the station we are meant to reach, but instead the terminals we find ourselves in that will bring to light how to get there. What matters is the journey itself and only that manifested through experiences. During our voyage, we connect with others and become united through the energetic power of the universe.

This teaches us how to feel, to open our hearts to love and to be kind to one another, so that we can embrace the unique moments we are here to live with each person we may meet. We encounter challenges that bring out the fear in us not so that we give up, but to remind us that we are human beings and that the only way to grow is to be grateful and conquer the struggles, because always from darkness, the light will appear. Throughout this adventure we are faced with choices that can completely shake up our foundations, so that we can continue to rebuild and to find our inner self. We learn how brave we are by falling and learning to get up again. The more we do this, the less it starts to hurt. From suffering, we open our hearts to compassion and to understand that everything that is broken can be healed again. We identify that nurturing ourselves and others is what we can offer one another, because we all share this beautiful characteristic. It is one with the soul and we all have that. But most importantly, we learn to keep on walking because ultimately at some point, we will discover ourselves, awaken our senses and acknowledge our authenticity. And when this happens, we are faced to see the reflection of all that's been waiting to be revealed to us. It's always been there, within, walking on this long road with us as the perfect companion.

It is that deeper side of our self that has been guiding the steps, so that one day, we can become one and see that we are compete and always have been. We know this because it is how it all started, with the end. And as we reach the point to acknowledge this, we awaken to the possibility that we are here for the sole purpose of living as the original self, in the purest way possible, so when our soul returns through another physical dimension, it will continue to further explore what we had left uncovered with the experiences gained along its journey so far.

LAST WORDS

In the beginning, we all know the end. I knew mine at 7 years old when I started writing poetry; at fifteen when I was the top student in the English class; in my late teens when I began my blog and during my public relations career when I was writing articles for magazines and publications. I knew it then and somehow, I just forgot. But alongside all the bumpy rides I have been on and every single side street that I took, they all led me to find myself again; to rediscover my soul's purest intention and why I am here. Without any of the experiences I had encountered, I wouldn't have been able to reach this point.

But most importantly, I had awakened myself to the possibility of love, kindness and a sense of adventure towards my life, not driven by achieving states of personal satisfaction, but instead living in the moment, appreciating that I don't need to become somebody, for I am already that somebody, just like everybody else is.

You know what your life purpose is. We all do, and yes, we can definitely forget but we will also be reminded of it. Life happens for us because we choose the actions we take; we are the creators of our journey and we can do anything we set our minds to so long as the soul always leads. Everything you have gone through in your life and continue to do so are all experiences that will lead you to that point you are searching for, consciously or unconsciously. It is all part of the soul's quest on the physical dimension to bring you closer to your true self, to find that genius within you and to share your own gift with the world, with the way you can serve the world. The most important thing to take in consideration is that you can become and live as your most original self. Listen to your intuition, look out for signs and always seek the truth from within. Only then you will be given the clarity you need to continue with your life mission. And when you happen to take a wrong turn, because you will, know that it will lead you back to where you were supposed to be in the first place.

Wrong turns are simply detours to teach us the lessons we have failed to learn whilst on the path. Because life is a miracle and we are the lucky ones to experience it all. Some say that it's not about the fortunes you gain or the milestones you acquire throughout your life that make you happy. All these things have given you the possibility to feel happy at one point. And although that feeling didn't last, it certainly taught you how to identify it and most importantly how it feels. When external influences bring you joy, let them.

They all have their reasoning and the meaning you take from them is simply your own perception of it and until you truly understand this, you will not appreciate your greatness, your soul's purpose. You see what you want to see and this all starts with your intention and what is going on internally for you. Everything from within will show itself on the outside and the way we react will sometimes be from the fear of facing what we don't want to face. But this in itself is a miracle because once we learn that what we fear is non-existent externally, but simply self-created from our ego's need to protect, we can break down these walls and live with more clarity. Do what feels right for you so long you keep true to yourself and have good intentions. Whatever you create let it shine and learn to do it even better so that you can reach the next phase in your path. But ultimately your legacy is left from how you have grown as an individual and how you best cooperated with the soul you have come to live as.

Once you are internally at peace with this, you will manifest the same externally. You are what your soul is, and your soul is one with you. Your body is simply a vessel that transports it through time on the physical dimension. With every lesson learnt you take a step closer to your rediscovery. Some experiences are not there to bring us joy, but instead to open us to strength, bravery and courage. Your soul will continue to live on and what matters is how you experience its existence within you in your lifetime.

LIST OF AFFIRMATIONS

SELF-BELIEF

I believe that I am worthy and capable of manifesting my own genius.

I respect myself enough to know that I can rely on myself to make things happen.

I believe in myself because I know that my existence is significant and needed.

I am responsible for my own actions and I choose to believe that I deserve to live as my most original self.

BODY LOVE

I love and appreciate my body and I give it the right foods and exercise to that it can perform better.

I deserve to live a healthy, happy, active lifestyle.

I exercise because I love and appreciate my body and overall wellness.

I live a healthy life because it's important to me.

I feel energized and productive every day because I live an active, healthy lifestyle.

DAILY AFFIRMATIONS

Today is a great day and I am grateful for being part of it.

Today I make the conscious decision to live from authenticity and appreciate all that is around me.

Success is already within me and I am complete the way I am.

I am grateful for today and I am going to make it count.

I let go of any expectations and instead will take today as it comes because good things are on their way to me.

I honour myself completely and respect every part of my being.

ABOUT THE AUTHOR

Miriam is a published writer, yoga teacher and qualified NLP (neuro-linguistic programming) Practitioner with an academic background in Psychology, focusing on behaviour, effective goal setting and strategies for self-development. Passionate about health and holistic medicine, Miriam also gained her Ayurveda diploma, specializing in health consultations, Abhyanga, Marma Therapy and Shirodhara body treatments. Additionally, she completed studies in Chinese medicine, Body Language and Reflexology. She is the creator of <u>Self-Elevation.com</u> online platform for empowering people to achieve their greatness.

www.ingramcontent.com/pod-product-compliance
Lightning Source LLC
Chambersburg PA
CBHW071924290426
44110CB00013B/1469